Creating Hysteria

Creating Hysteria

Women and Multiple Personality Disorder

Joan Acocella

Jossey-Bass Publishers
San Francisco

Jossey-Bass books and products are available through most bookstores. To contact Jossey-Bass directly, call (888) 378-2537, fax to (800) 605-2665, or visit our website at www.josseybass.com.

Substantial discounts on bulk quantities of Jossey-Bass books are available to corporations, professional associations, and other organizations. For details and discount information, contact the special sales department at Jossey-Bass.

TCF Manufactured in the United States of America on Lyons Falls Turin Book. This paper is acid-free and 100 percent totally chlorine-free.

Library of Congress Cataloging-in-Publication Data

Acocella, Joan Ross.
  Creating hysteria : women and multiple personality disorder / Joan Acocella. — 1st ed.
  p.   cm.
  Includes bibliographical references (p. 179) and index.
  ISBN 0-7879-4794-6
  1. Multiple personality. 2. False memory syndrome. I. Title.
  RC569.5.M8 A28   1999
  616.85'236'0082—dc21   99–6358

HB Printing   10 9 8 7 6 5 4 3 2 1   FIRST EDITION

To Stephen Kirschner

Contents

1

One Woman's Story

In late 1989 Elizabeth Carlson, a thirty-five-year-old woman who lived with her husband and two children in a Minneapolis suburb, was in the hospital being treated for severe depression. She was referred to a psychiatrist, Diane Humenansky, who came to see her, and went on seeing her after she left the hospital. As Carlson recalls, Humenansky soon suggested to her that perhaps her problem was not depression but multiple personality disorder. MPD, Humenansky explained, was an elusive illness: many diagnosticians failed to recognize the alternating personalities, or alters, for what they were. As a result, many women—nine out of ten MPs were women[1]—ended up getting misdiagnosed. But experts now knew that there were certain telltale signs of MPD. Did Carlson ever "zone out" while driving and arrive at her destination without remembering quite how she got there? Why, yes, Carlson said. Well, that was an alter taking over the driving and then vanishing again, leaving her, the "host" personality, to account for the blackout. Another sign of MPD, Humenansky said, was "voices in the head." Did Carlson ever have internal arguments—for example, telling herself, "Turn right" and then, "No, turn left"? Yes, Carlson replied, that happened sometimes. Well, that was the alters fighting with each other inside her head.

Carlson was amazed and embarrassed. All these years, she had done these things, never realizing that they were symptoms of a serious mental disorder.

Multiple personality, Humenansky went on to explain, was associated with childhood sexual abuse, though the abuse might be forgotten. Carlson should think hard: had anyone ever taken liberties with her? Carlson didn't have to think hard. She distinctly remembered being molested as a child by two different men in her family. She had never forgotten these episodes. That didn't mean she hadn't forgotten other episodes, Humenansky said. Worse ones, maybe.

To help Carlson remember, Humenansky gave her books to read. One was *The Courage to Heal* by Ellen Bass and Laura Davis, which had just come out—the book now known as the Bible of the recovered memory movement. One-third of American women were survivors of childhood sexual abuse, *The Courage to Heal* declared, though many did not remember the abuse. If a girl was repeatedly molested, she might have not only suppressed the memory but developed separate personalities in which to seal off the terrible knowledge. The book explained this theory of multiple personality disorder, and gave first-person accounts. In a later edition, one woman wrote:

> I remember splitting for the first time when I was four
> and my father was trying to force me to sodomize my pet
> rabbit with a roofing nail. He got very angry when I
> refused, and finally, in a rage, he threw me down on the
> basement floor and raped me. When I came back to
> myself after the experience, there were three parts of
> me. . . . They were Benjamin—ageless, spiritual and pro-
> tective; Bunny—little and worried; and Scarlet, the only
> female and the one who dealt with the sexual abuse.[2]

Humenansky also gave Carlson books about MPD cases. One was Corbett Thigpen and Hervey Cleckley's 1957 *The Three Faces of Eve*, the story of a shy, depressed housewife, "Eve White," who, on the odd weekend, would metamorphose into "Eve Black," a vivacious party girl, leaving her host personality with unexplained hangovers and a reputation in local bars. Between this book and the

1957 movie based on it, featuring an Academy Award–winning performance by Joanne Woodward, Eve became, for a while, the prototype of the multiple personality. In later cases, as in Eve's, there was usually the good–bad split—"librarian by day and streetwalker by night," to quote MPD expert Frank Putnam.[3] Later multiples, like Eve, also tended to show asymmetrical amnesia, with the "good" personality remaining ignorant of the activities of the "bad" one while the latter knew all about her prim counterpart and enjoyed making her life hell.

Eve, however, was merely the John the Baptist of multiple personality; the Christ was "Sybil Dorsett," a Columbia University graduate student who in 1954, at age thirty-one, turned up in the office of a psychoanalyst named Cornelia Wilbur and stayed for eleven years. In 1973 this case became the subject of a mass-market book, *Sybil*, by the journalist Flora Rheta Schreiber. Three years later the book was turned into a gripping TV movie with Sally Field as Sybil and with Joanne Woodward, passing the torch, as Dr. Wilbur. The book was a best-seller; the movie won four Emmy awards. Sybil became the most famous psychiatric patient in history, and her manifestation of what Wilbur called multiple personality disorder became the pattern of the disorder, in a form substantially different from Eve's. For one thing, MPD now had a clear cause: childhood abuse. Eve had suffered traumas as a child, but she was never sexually assaulted. Sybil was, repeatedly, by her mother. Furthermore, the mother's actions were sadistic, perverse, extravagant. According to the book, she probed the child's vagina with a knife and a buttonhook. She hung her upside-down and, using an enema bag, filled her bladder with ice-cold water. Then she tied her to the family piano and forbade her to urinate while she, the mother, sat down and played Chopin.

Second, Sybil had a dissociation history worthy of her abuse history. As described by her therapists, Eve had had only three faces. (Eves White and Black were later joined by a Jane.) Sybil had sixteen personalities, keyed to specific traumas. There was Ruthie, a

3

baby, who split off upon watching her parents have sex. There was Peggy Lou, who came out when Sybil's grandmother died. One personality played the piano; another could install sheet-rock; two had English accents; two were men. Sybil wasn't so much a person as a club.

With this case the disorder not only changed, it spread. Prior to Sybil, MPD had been one of the rarest of mental disorders. In a 1944 article two researchers, W. S. Taylor and Mabel Martin, reported that a search of the medical literature of the nineteenth and twentieth centuries had yielded only seventy-six cases that met their definition. But after Sybil, MPD exploded. One expert estimates that between 1985 and 1995 there were almost 40,000 new cases. And curiously, the latter-day multiples looked a lot like Sybil. The modal MPD patient, experts reported, was a white North American female around age thirty. As with Sybil, her disorder had begun in childhood, flowering into a large constellation of alters. In one study of 236 cases, the mean number of alters was sixteen, Sybil's count exactly.[4] And whereas early sexual trauma had not been reported in a single one of the Taylor and Martin cases, most of the new multiples, like Sybil, said they had suffered child abuse, usually including sexual abuse.

Actually, in both these respects, Sybil's descendants soon outstripped her. Patients were eventually producing a hundred, four hundred, a thousand alters. (A case with forty-five hundred was recently reported.) And whereas Sybil had confined herself to human alters, later MPs branched out. In a Wisconsin malpractice case that was settled in 1977 for $2.4 million, the patient claimed that among the 126 alters she developed in MPD therapy there were several angels, a duck, and "Lillith," the bride of Satan. The Georgia-based psychiatrist George Ganaway, one of the first authorities to caution against fascination with MPD, reported that he had been presented with "sages, lobsters, chickens, tigers, a gorilla, a unicorn, and 'God.'"[5]

In abuse too, Sybil was rapidly outdone. Reports of child rape and sodomy were common. Truddi Chase, author of the MPD memoir *When Rabbit Howls*, recounts that her stepfather used to lower her down a well and throw live snakes on top of her. In this efflorescence of abuse reports, an important contributor was "satanic ritual abuse," or SRA, which spread to MPD from the day-care scandals of the early 1980s. Now MPs were claiming that they had been molested not just by individuals working on their own but by multigenerational cults of Satan-worshipers who met by night to rape young girls and thereby breed babies. On other nights, the cult members aborted, stabbed, skinned, and ate the babies, while wearing hooded garments. These Satanic cults created MPD not just in the usual way, by traumatizing the child and thus causing her to split. Through sophisticated brainwashing techniques, they deliberately programmed her with task-specific alters, who, as in *The Manchurian Candidate*, would carry out assignments—usually murder, sometimes suicide—at the bidding of the cult.

Another area in which the new multiples left their forerunners in the dust was self-destructiveness. Eve had considered suicide; Sybil too was suicidal and would occasionally put her fist through a window. But the MPs of the eighties and nineties were more ingenious. In one popular MPD biography, *Suffer the Child*, the subject pours drain cleaner on her genitals. A former multiple interviewed in Mark Pendergrast's *Victims of Memory* tells him that she began pulling her toenails off: "I didn't feel anything. I would rip the whole nail right off, blood all over the place." Other multiples have shown journalists their self-inflicted cuts, their third-degree burns. Self-mutilation was accepted by many MPD writers as a regular feature of the disorder, a "coping mechanism." In the words of MPD expert Colin Ross, "Every time you cut, you're working on trying to keep the body safe." Starting in 1990, self-mutilators—a group that includes many kinds of patients, not just MPs—had a newsletter, *The Cutting Edge*, that they could subscribe to. In a 1996 issue

"Carla" writes in that she doesn't really want to stop cutting her-self and that her new therapist has left the decision up to her. So she's cutting again, "yet it's been a time of tremendous growth and potential."[6]

As the number of MPD patients grew, so, naturally, did the field designated to treat them. Until about 1975, there had been no MPD specialty to speak of. Multiple personality disorder had no separate listing in the American Psychiatric Association's *Diagnostic and Statistical Manual of Mental Disorders*, or *DSM*, the guidebook to diagnosis. The condition was simply mentioned in passing as a subtype of "hysterical neurosis." But in 1980, after strenuous lobbying by interested therapists, the new edition of *DSM* gave multiple personality disorder a primary-level listing among the dissociative disorders, conditions in which some part of mental functioning splits off from consciousness. MPD was now a full-fledged psychiatric syndrome. In 1984 the new MPD enthusiasts founded an organization of their own, the International Society for the Study of Multiple Personality and Dissociation (ISSMP&D), and began holding annual conferences, cosponsored by Rush-Presbyterian-St. Luke's Medical Center in Chicago and chaired by MPD expert Bennett Braun. Rush-Presbyterian subsequently opened the country's first dissociative disorders (DD) unit, under Braun. Other units followed. The field soon had its own journal, *Dissociation*, which began publication in 1988. By 1990 the average annual output of publications on MPD had multiplied 6,000 percent over the pre-1970 level.[7]

Among those publications were two comprehensive textbooks, Frank Putnam's *Diagnosis and Treatment of Multiple Personality Disorder* and Colin Ross's *Multiple Personality Disorder* (both 1989), from which one could learn how to recognize and treat MPD. Both books offered the same theory of the disorder, the theory that Wilbur had offered for Sybil. (It is called the "Wilburian paradigm.") The cause of MPD was trauma, usually abuse, usually including sexual molestation. In order to cope, the child imagined that the abuse was happening to someone else, another "her," who then split off from the main personality, growing in isolation behind a wall of amnesia—a process called dissociation. As dissociation occurred again and again, the personalities multiplied, each developing its own name, nature, and function and typically remaining the age it was when it first appeared.

Both Putnam and Ross published surveys claiming to demonstrate the correlation between MPD and childhood abuse, and both, in their textbooks, offered treatment plans focusing on the abuse. Clearly, if forgotten trauma was the cause, the cure was to remember and come to terms with the trauma. The therapist had to flush out the alters and get them to divulge their secrets, in protracted reenactments called *abreactions*. In a typical abreaction, as Colin Ross described it, the patient might "cry out, plead with the father to stop, clutch her pubic area, try to push the father off, attempt to spit out semen, or curl up in a corner." These were violent scenes. (David Calof, an MPD-treater, reports that one of his patients had a stroke during an abreaction.) Ross warned that abreactions should not be allowed to go on too long, but others were less conservative. Bennett Braun said he had having supervised nine-hour abreactions.[8]

Obviously, the rise in the number of MPD cases boosted the growth of the MPD specialty. And vice versa. George Ganaway recalls that when he went to his first ISSMP&D conference in 1985, most of those attending, apart from the speakers, had seen perhaps one or two cases of MPD. But what they learned at that conference caused them, when they went home, to view their patients in a new light. "And when we came back the next year," Ganaway says, "we each had many more MPD patients to talk about."[9] In addition to what they picked up at conferences, they had the swelling MPD literature to inform them.

This, apparently, is how Diane Humenansky, Elizabeth Carlson's therapist, learned about multiple personality disorder. She read the experts—Putnam, Ross, Braun—together with *Sybil*. She spoke to Cornelia Wilbur. She attended an ISSMP&D conference. And eventually she had a number of newly diagnosed multiples under her care. Humenansky declined to be interviewed by me on the subject of Carlson; therefore my account of her treatment of Carlson is based on Carlson's description of it, supplemented by court records. It is hard to know what Humenansky was thinking, or indeed if she was in a position to practice psychotherapy in a responsible manner. Carlson says Humenansky told her she had been through three divorces, had lost custody of her children to her third husband, and was taking antidepressants. Nevertheless, when she began treating Carlson, Humenansky was a fully accredited physician—a graduate of Wayne State Medical School, though, according to Carlson, she claimed it was Harvard—with admitting privileges at several Twin Cities hospitals.

Carlson says Humenansky gave her not just books but videotapes too: the movie versions of *Sybil* and *The Three Faces of Eve*, talk shows featuring survivors of childhood torture. She told Carlson that if she felt any physical discomfort—anxiety, chills—while watching the videos, that was a "body memory": it meant that these things had happened to her too. According to Carlson, Humenansky also had her do visualization exercises, "trying on" scenes of being molested by people in her family. Using this technique, Carlson soon recovered memories of being molested by as many as fifty relatives, including both parents, both sets of grandparents, aunts, uncles, and great-grandparents.

She began having horrifying dreams. The dreams too were memories, Humenansky said. In their therapy sessions she would have Carlson abreact the remembered scene. If Carlson came into the therapy session with no memories, that meant she was "stuck," and Humenansky gave her more videos: pornographic movies, war footage of people being decapitated.

According to Carlson, Humenansky also used a method called guided imagery, in which the patient is talked through an imaginary scene in order to awaken buried memories. In one scenario Humenansky told Carlson to picture herself going downstairs. Look for an altar, Humenansky said. Carlson saw a stone slab. Look around for candles and daggers, Humenansky said, Carlson saw them. Now look for the baby, Humenansky said. Carlson does not remember at what point her own imagination, primed by the books and videos, took over, but soon she saw a pregnant woman, and then the baby was born, and then the afterbirth was sitting on the altar, and people in hooded robes were eating it, and so was she. (That was the first of many cannibalism scenes Carlson recovered with Dr. Humenansky. Today, she still has nightmares about them.) The therapy sessions often ended with Carlson weeping uncontrollably. Carlson says Humenansky would give her tranquilizers and tell her to chew them, so that they would take effect faster.

At the same time that Carlson, under Humenansky's guidance, was recalling the abuse that caused her personality to split, the two of them were also "mapping the system"—that is, identifying the different personalities. Ever since *Sybil* it had been accepted that any moderately elaborated MP system was likely to include child alters. Carlson obligingly dug up hers. One was Little Miss Fluff, a nickname that she had been given as a girl because she liked frilly dresses and crinolines. Another was Suzarina: that had been her imaginary playmate when she was a child, and it was decided that the playmate must have been an early alter. To fill the Eve-Black slot, Carlson came up with Wild Child, a teenage tramp, and Nikita, a more mature temptress. *Sybil* had had two male alters; so, quite soon, did Carlson. She also located two nuns, Sister Mary Margaret and Sister Mary Theresa (the latter wanted to join the Peace Corps), and a scared, depressed old lady called the Old Lady.

Some of these alters were discovered through "journaling," a technique recommended by MPD experts. Carlson was told to keep a journal; then, going over it, Humenansky picked out recurrent thoughts and identified them as alters, or as traces of abuse memories. When Carlson's mood changed—indeed, when she changed her hair or clothing style—Humenansky told her she had "switched," or changed alters. If she showed up for her session in a short skirt, that meant Nikita was "out." If she was depressed, that was the Old Lady taking over. With each new personality they unearthed, Carlson was asked to supply the name, but if she drew a blank, Humenansky did the naming.

In the middle of the treatment, according to Carlson, Humenansky went to the ISSMP&D conference in Chicago and returned with the news that MPs also tended to have lesbian, animal, and devil personalities. Carlson thereupon produced something that growled and that they figured was either an animal or a devil. She also came up with a lesbian alter. Humenansky urged her to get in touch with this side of herself, so Carlson went to a strip club with a lesbian friend, got drunk, and tried, with little success, to have sex with her.

Interestingly, though—and this seems to be the case with a number of MPs who have not yet written memoirs—Carlson never quite got the hang of multiplicity. To this day, she doesn't know how many personalities she had. "After twenty-five, I lost count," she says. Humenansky had Carlson write down their names, ages, and key memories on index cards for reference. Still, Carlson says, "I couldn't keep the darn things straight." Once, she lost the card file, and they had to do the whole thing all over again.

There were times when she would walk into Humenansky's office and say that she didn't want to recover memories or explore alters that day. She just needed to talk. She recalls:

> Dr. Humenansky said, "Well, who am I talking to?" And I would say, "This is just me." She said, "No, I want to know which alter I'm talking to." "It's not an alter," I said. "It's just me." Finally she got out an index card and wrote down, "Just Me."

Later, Carlson says, Humenansky put her under sodium amytal ("truth serum") and asked her, "OK, who's the 'Just Me' person?"

Meanwhile, Carlson's mental condition was worsening. The main events of her week were her two appointments with Humenansky, one individual session and one meeting with a group that Humenansky led for her MPD patients. For a year, she was so depressed that she rarely left her bedroom. She hung blankets over the windows, so that the room was always dark. She wore a flannel nightgown and huddled under piles of blankets. Heavily drugged, she sometimes slept eighteen to twenty hours a day. She woke up screaming from nightmares and went into fits of projectile vomiting. "I stank, the room stank. Every few days or so, my husband or my daughter would take me and shove me into the shower and hose me down." Then she would go back to bed.

Carlson's daughter Lisha, who was in her teens, took over the household and the care of her younger brother. Eventually, she had to drop out of school. Carlson's marriage, which had already been troubled when she began seeing Humenansky, deteriorated day by day. Carlson says Humenansky suggested that perhaps her husband, David, was trying to kill her. Carlson threw him out of the house repeatedly. Meanwhile, she had cut off all contact with the rest of her family because, as she now understood from her therapy, they were still members of the cult that had abused her as a child, and if they found out what she was revealing in therapy, they would murder her. She couldn't even answer her telephone when it rang, because if the caller was a cult member, he or she could say a key word that would trigger the emergence of a homicidal alter, and then Carlson would kill somebody, perhaps her husband or children.

On Humenansky's recommendation, Carlson now and then checked into the hospital—a situation that, according to the guidelines of Social Security Disability, which was paying for her therapy (Humenansky had arranged this), justified more frequent therapy sessions. Humenansky told her not to mention her cult history to the hospital staff; if she did, the cult would find out that Humenansky was trying to unmask them and would come after her. Once Carlson slipped. A Catholic priest visited her room, and she told him about her cult memories, adding that she felt she was possessed and needed an exorcism. The priest said that she didn't need an exorcism; she needed a new therapist. Leaving out the last part, Carlson happily reported to Humenansky that the priest thought her cult memories were imaginary. Humenansky answered that of course he would say that: the Catholic church was in alliance with the cults. Wasn't Carlson's own cult-ridden family Catholic?

"I just got crazier and crazier," Carlson says. She banged her head on walls and tore out her hair in chunks. "I was ready to kill myself. I thought it was better for me, and better for my children." When, in rare moments of protest, she asked Humenansky why the therapy wasn't helping, the doctor repeated to her a basic principle of MPD treatment: the patient has to get worse in order to get better.

⫸ ⫷

How could these things have happened? How could Carlson have believed what Humenansky was telling her? According to Carlson and others now repudiating MPD and recovered-memory treatment—they are called "retractors"—it is not hard, given certain circumstances. One is drugs. MPD patients are often given strong medications, particularly benzodiazepines such as Valium, Halcion, and Xanax for anxiety and insomnia. "I have found that MPD patients can tolerate enormous doses of benzodiazepines," writes Colin Ross enthusiastically in his textbook on the disorder. (In a 1995 court case Ross acknowledged that he had put one patient on fifty-one milligrams of Halcion a day, which is *one hundred times* the prescribed maximum for that drug.) Sequentially or simultaneously, Carlson, during her time with Humenansky, took Xanax, Valium, and Ativan for anxiety; Pamelor, Desyrel, and Prozac for depression; and Restoril for insomnia, often in heavy doses. In the words of one retractor, "If you take enough drugs, you can remember about anything."[10]

A second factor is hypnosis, which has often been used to obtain the information—the alters, the abuse history—that leads to the MPD diagnosis. Already in the nineteenth century it was recognized that the memories that people retrieved under hypnosis, however

12

detailed or convincing, were not necessarily accurate. Later research has confirmed this again and again. To quote a 1985 American Medical Association report, "recollections obtained during hypnosis . . . actually appear to be less reliable than nonhypnotic recall." Furthermore, those recollections are exquisitely sensitive to cuing by the hypnotist. This too has been known for a long time. In the words of the nineteenth-century hypnosis authority Hippolyte Bernheim, "When a physician employs hypnosis with a patient, it is wise always to be aware of who may be hypnotizing whom." Experiments have shown that hypnotized subjects, given the appropriate suggestion, can recall former lives as chimpanzees.[11]

Nor does the suggestion have to be stated as fact; a question will suffice. In one experiment, reported in 1983, twenty-seven people were hypnotized, taken back to a night during the preceding week, and asked whether, on that night, they had been awakened by a loud noise. Seventeen of them, almost two-thirds of the group, said yes. And when they were brought out of the trance, thirteen of them continued to believe that they had had this experience—which illustrates another principle of hypnosis: that regardless of the accuracy of the memory, hypnosis increases the subject's confidence in it. For these reasons, courts in about half the states no longer admit hypnotically refreshed testimony. But the message has been slow in getting through to the profession that most often employs hypnosis. In 1992, in a survey of over a thousand psychotherapists with advanced degrees, hypnosis expert Michael Yapko found that almost half believed that memories produced under hypnosis were more accurate than nonhypnotic recall. Indeed, one-fourth believed that hypnosis could recover accurate memories of past lives.[12]

According to a number of experts in the dissociative disorders, that faith in hypnotic recall on the part of the therapist was one of the central pillars supporting the MPD movement. Another crucial factor was high hypnotizability on the part of the patient. The ability to go into a trance varies from person to person, but as MPD experts themselves point out, it doesn't vary that much in MPs. As a group, they are exceedingly hypnotizable. They enter trances easily; they accept suggestions readily. The MPD people point this up as an interesting fact about MPs. What they do not seem to understand is that high hypnotizability is likely to be the interesting fact that *got* these patients diagnosed as MPs. Imagine that a highly hypnotizable woman goes to a therapist who believes in MPD and in the accuracy of hypnotic recall. Imagine, then, that the therapist asks her, while she is under hypnosis, whether she has other "parts" to her personality—something that most of us feel we have, if only metaphorically (our rational self, our irrational self; our adult self, our child self). Imagine, finally, that the therapist asks her whether she wasn't abused as a child—something that many of us feel we were, if only psychologically, and which some of us were literally. The patient is likely to produce.

When confronted with this scenario, MPD believers protest that many patients reveal their alters and receive their diagnosis without having been formally hypnotized. But high-hypnotizables do not require formal hypnotic induction in order to go into a trance. Guided imagery will do the job, as will relaxation techniques and other forms of suggestion. Furthermore, many women diagnosed as MPs need no suggestion whatsoever. Whether or not they have multiple personality disorder, a large number of them do seem to have dissociative symptoms—amnesias, "spells," transient feelings that they are not real or that the world is not real. "In some sense," Colin Ross writes, "my patients probably go into trance walking across the hospital parking lot to get to our building."[13]

It is this trance-proneness that makes them unusually vulnerable to suggestion. In a case reported in the *New Yorker* in 1993 by Lawrence Wright, Paul Ingram, a trance-prone man who had been accused of molesting his daughters, was told by Richard Ofshe, a social psychologist specializing in mind control, that one of the girls was now claiming that Ingram had forced her to have sex with her brother. The story was not true—Ofshe was performing an experiment—but Ingram came to believe it was true. The next day he presented Ofshe with a three-page account, in vivid detail, of how he had made the children have intercourse and had watched. Likewise Elizabeth Carlson remembered in detail the meetings of her family's satanic cult: how the men had beards and wore brown capes, how they aborted the woman's baby and then laid the afterbirth on the altar and started eating it. To obtain this memory, Humenansky did not hypnotize Carlson and didn't have to. Guided imagery sufficed, for Carlson is highly trance-prone.

Another important circumstance in Carlson's case, as in other MPD histories, was the media. During the period of Carlson's therapy, magazines and newspapers were retailing utterly unbelievable stories about MPD. So was the evening news. MPD experts went on TV with their patients in tow. Bennett Braun, of the nine-hour abreactions, appeared on the Chicago evening news with his star patient. At his bidding she "switched" on camera—now she was "Sarah," now "Pete"—thus providing early training for prospective MPs in the television audience.

More important than the news were the talk shows. Phil Donahue was apparently the first talk-show host to present a program on MPD; he was followed by Sally Jessy Raphael, Larry King, Leeza Gibbons, and Oprah Winfrey. Meanwhile, celebrities were coming forward with their tales of childhood sexual abuse: Roseanne Barr, La Toya Jackson, Oprah herself. Some of them claimed to be multiples as well. Roseanne, who had unearthed twenty-one personalities within herself—Piggy, Bambi, and Fucker, among others—made the rounds. Again and again on the talk shows it was stressed that MPD was not rare; it was common, and becoming more so. "This could be someone you know," said Sally Jessy Raphael. Oprah's program was called "MPD: The Syndrome of the '90s."[14] Today, as people are sifting through the wreckage created by the MPD movement, many therapists are blaming the media for spreading the epidemic. They are passing the buck, but still they have a point.

Apart from publicity, another factor that drew women into MPD therapy was of course unhappiness. If Carlson did not undergo satanic ritual abuse as a child, she suffered plenty of ordinary abuse. She came from a family with eight children and a distraught mother. "I believed that that was how all families were," she says. "That if your mother was having a bad day, she beat the crap out of you, bit you, took the belt to you, because you didn't do something as fast as you were supposed to." As for being molested, Carlson thought that was normal too, and when she found out it wasn't, she figured it was her fault: "Because I was such a girly girl, always flouncing around, with the little anklets and the little ringlets, and making the little tea party. I had called attention to myself, and that's how those incidents happened to me." At fourteen, she became rebellious and started running away from home. Then she lapsed into a depression, for which she was hospitalized and given electroshock treatment. Her parents, feeling unable to cope with her, made her a ward of the state, and she was placed in a "youth center." There followed many episodes of depression, together with suicide attempts.

By 1989, when Carlson began seeing Dr. Humenansky, she was on her second marriage, and it was failing. She had two children and no money. (She had sometimes worked as a fitness instructor, but at this point she had been unemployed for four years.) She had tried to go back to college, but in the middle of class she would be seized by a panic attack and would have to leave the room. She was in the hospital again—this was her fifth psychiatric hospitalization, as she recalls—when she was referred to Diane Humenansky. And when Humenansky told her that the cause of all her unhappiness was multiple personality disorder, her life made sense to her for the first time in many years. She felt she had failed in many ways, but now, it seemed, this wasn't her fault: "They tell you that somebody *else* did these horrible things to you, and that's why you are the person you are." Even in the present, her shortcomings were not hers.

It wasn't she who bolted out of classrooms in the grip of a panic attack; it was the Old Lady, who frightened so easily.

Finally, with the MPD diagnosis came the promise of a cure. As Humenansky explained, the reason no treatment had ever worked for Carlson before was that she had been treated for the wrong disorder. Now that her MPD had been identified, she could receive appropriate therapy, and her alters, giving up their secrets, would fuse into one personality. This therapy worked, Humenansky said, and many authorities had said so before her. Furthermore, it promised to be interesting. Just as with psychoanalysis, which is a direct ancestor of MPD therapy, the idea of going to the bottom of oneself, of finding out what really happened, sounds very brave. It also sounds efficient, like solving a crime—"a whodunit of the unconscious," as Flora Rheta Schreiber called the case of Sybil.[15] You find the criminal, and then everything can go back to normal. In *The Three Faces of Eve*, that is exactly how it works. Eve has a culminating traumatic memory, screams like a banshee, and fuses on the spot.

MPD therapy offers a further inducement, political solidarity. Child molesting is primarily a crime against females, and that, according to MPD insiders, is why MPD has been so ignored in the past, because women had no political power. To own up to one's abuse, to reveal the damage done—in short, to have MPD—is to stand up for women. Humenansky said that she was going to write a book on MPD, and that Carlson's story would be part of it. Carlson was joining a vanguard. They also talked about Carlson's going into the business: "I would have my therapeutic family, Dr. Humenansky and the group, and then I would become a therapist, with her. She would oversee things, and I would do therapy, to help other multiples." Indeed, Carlson had a therapeutic family already, Humenansky's MPD group. At their meetings, the women would get down on the floor, switch into their child personalities, and play board games, while Humenansky sat in a chair smiling down on them—like Mother Goose, Carlson says. "There we'd be, playing Candyland, and our insurance companies would be getting charged for it!"

To this machinery of causes, add one last element, fear. Carlson says that when she was not responding to Humenansky's therapy as she was supposed to—when she failed to come up with new alters, new abuse memories—the doctor reminded her that patients who undermined their own treatment and thereby failed to get better could have their children removed to foster care. (Carlson's children were not David Carlson's. They were from earlier unions.) According to Carlson, another woman in Humenansky's MPD group had had her son removed temporarily, on the doctor's recommendation. Humenansky also mentioned the possibility of Carlson's going to the state mental hospital. Such threats are not uncommon in MPD therapy, and they have added force in that MPD patients often feel they are doing poorly as mothers—which, as they sink into the grip of this therapy, is often the case. Some have been persuaded to bring their children in for therapy too. Carlson's daughter Lisha was in treatment with Humenansky for over a year, but the girl never embraced the therapy the way Elizabeth did. She was too frightened by what it was doing to her mother. According to Lisha, Humenansky told her she had reason to fear: the illness was genetic.

Eventually, Carlson came to her senses, almost by accident, or two accidents. After she had been in treatment for a year and a half, a friend in her MPD group recommended to her a new medication. She got a prescription from Humenansky, started taking the drug, and felt better, so she flushed all the other pills down the toilet. Around the same time, a problem arose in the MPD group. Humenansky brought in a new patient, and nobody liked her. "She monopolized the hour," Carlson says. "No one else could talk. Also, she kept lifting up her blouse and showing us where she had sprayed oven cleaner on herself. It was horrible, all pus and scabs." When the others protested, Humenansky told them that if they didn't like the group the way it was, they could start their own group. They did. Once a week, they got together, and as they talked in Humenansky's absence, they began to notice certain odd things: all of them had similar abuse memories, memories that furthermore closely resembled events in the books Humenansky had given them to read. Carlson recalls: "One woman said, 'I have a confession to make. I made up an alter named Nikki because everybody else in the group had a Nikki and I felt left out.' Slowly it began to dawn on us, what had happened. And then things changed. We started keeping secrets from Dr. Humenansky. But I didn't feel I could quit therapy. I was afraid of her. Also, a lot of the time, I still felt I needed her."

Then one day Carlson called Humenansky's office to confirm an appointment. As she recalls, Humenansky told her "that the MPD group was conspiring against her and that she was dropping all of us as patients, on the advice of her attorneys. This was in November. I begged her to keep me until the holidays were over. Christmas was always hard for me. She said no and hung up. I cried. That was the end. Two years."

※ ※

Carlson's is by no means the most grotesque of the MPD cases that have come to light in the past few years. A 1995 *Frontline* documentary, "The Search for Satan," written and produced by Ofra Bikel and Rachel Dretzin, told the story of Patricia Burgus, Bennett Braun's "star patient," the one who switched under his ministrations for the Chicago TV news. Burgus, who originally sought treatment for postpartum depression, was hospitalized for three years in Braun's dissociative disorders unit at Rush-Presbyterian. There, in the course of her therapy with Braun, she came to believe that she had more than three hundred personalities; that she had been raised by her family in a satanic cult (indeed, that she was a satanic priestess in charge of a nine-state region); that she had eaten more than two thousand dead bodies, in whole or in part, per year; that she had molested her two sons, John and Mikey; and that these two children, aged five and four, respectively, were cult members in their own right, and practiced killers.

At Braun's suggestion, Burgus allowed her sons to be hospitalized for approximately three years at Rush, where they were treated for MPD and debriefed by Braun and others as to their cult activities. (Braun was a firm believer in cult abuse.) The boys were given stickers as rewards for producing memories of murder and cannibalism. "The Search for Satan" reproduces hospital records of the therapy sessions—for example, "John recalled an incident where a black woman was seized by the cult and choked to death. Afterwards, victim was barbecued. Three stickers." On a later television documentary—"Devil's Advocate," aired on NBC's *Dateline* in 1998—Burgus tells how, in therapy, "Mikey had to talk about what it was like to eat the baby, to bite the baby while it was still alive." Burgus also reports that Braun had her husband bring back a hamburger from a picnic with her family so that it could be tested in the hospital laboratory for human tissue. According to Burgus, Braun called the FBI; agents came to the hospital, and Burgus reported her parents as cult murderers. When the agents refused to do anything about this, she says, Braun told her that the FBI had joined the conspiracy.

When Burgus's insurance coverage was almost exhausted, she was discharged from the hospital, though she had to go to court to get John and Mikey released. The family is still recovering from the experience. It took Burgus eight years to reconcile with her parents. As for the boys, John was being "mainstreamed" into a regular school—Mikey, however, was still in a special school—at the time when "The Search for Satan" was broadcast. The medical costs for Burgus and her sons to have this done to them were over $3 million.

There is worse. Burgus still has her family. That is not the case with Mary Shanley, an elementary school teacher who, having sought treatment for anxiety and depression, ended up in Rush North Shore Hospital in Skokie, in another dissociative disorders unit headed by Braun. There, under the care of Braun and his colleague Roberta Sachs, Shanley developed fifteen child alters plus seven alters who were members of a satanic cult. Under heavy drug therapy, she "confessed" that the cult killers were laying plans to murder her husband and her son, that they had already molested the son, and that she too had molested him.

According to Shanley, Sachs eventually called in a consultant, D. Corydon Hammond. Hammond has lectured widely on his theory that the mastermind of American cult activity is a German Jewish doctor, one Dr. Green (formerly Greenbaum), who collaborated with the Nazis and then escaped to the United States, where he developed a cult based on the Greek alphabet for programming cult inductees. Hammond questioned Shanley under hypnosis and decided that she needed to be deprogrammed. For this purpose she was transferred to the care of Judith Peterson, a clinical psychologist specializing in cult-induced MPD at a private psychiatric hospital, Spring Shadows Glen, in Houston. Shanley remained at Spring Shadows Glen for two years, at an average cost to her insurance company of $1,200 *per day*. On "The Search for Satan" we see a segment of a videotaped therapy session between Peterson and Shanley. Peterson is calling out the cult alters, asking them for the murder plan. "Who's going to kill Joe?" she demands. "Who'd you give the job to?" Shanley, in restraints, screams a scream from the bottom of hell.

Like the Burgus children, Shanley's son, age nine, was hospitalized along with his mother. The makers of "The Search for Satan" asked the hospital staff whether they felt there was anything wrong with this. One nurse answered that they did but that they learned to keep quiet: "It became very clear . . . that if we objected, there would be a reprisal and that reprisal would be a transfer off the unit, a demotion, in some cases an actual termination." According to another nurse, "If you resisted the psychologist or the psychiatrist, you might be labeled as one of the cult. And that happened to some people."

Shanley too has since recovered from her multiple personality disorder. As with Burgus, her insurance money finally ran out, and when she stopped receiving treatment for MPD, she stopped having MPD. But for five years she could not go back to teaching, because she was on record as a child abuser. (Peterson had reported her to the authorities.) Her husband, who was drawn into her therapy and believed that she was planning to murder him, divorced her. As of 1995, when "The Search for Satan" was aired, Shanley's son was in the father's custody and refused to see her, since she was not only plotting to kill him but had also molested him. Had she not said so herself?

These two cases differ from Carlson's not only in the extent of the damage but also in the standing of the professionals involved. Bennett Braun was not an ordinary practitioner like Diane Humenansky. He was the founding president of the ISSMP&D and the chair of its annual meetings in Chicago from their inception in 1984 through 1994. He established the DD unit at Rush, "the world's leading Dissociative Disorders unit," in the words of his colleague Colin Ross.[16] He also published one of the first MPD treatment plans. Peterson was clinical director of the dissociative disorders unit at Spring Shadows Glen. She and Roberta Sachs were recognized authorities on MPD, the authors of training programs for other therapists. D. Corydon Hammond was the first president of the American Society of Clinical Hypnosis. He was a professor at the University of Utah School of Medicine and the editor of a standard textbook on hypnosis. The Burgus and Shanley cases came not from the margins of the MPD movement but from top center.

∗≫ ≪∗

But if Carlson's case was not the most scandalous, it was still a landmark. In 1993 and 1994, Carlson and another woman in her MPD group, Vynette Hamanne, sued Diane Humenansky. Humenansky denied most of their allegations. At the Carlson trial she testified that she had complied with "the requisite standard of care in all respects." Nevertheless, Carlson was awarded $2.4 million in damages, and Hamanne $2.7 million. According to the women's attorneys, Edward Glennon, R. Christopher Barden, and Christopher Yetka, these were the largest jury verdicts ever delivered in the United States in a case involving recovered memory. They set an example. Nine other former patients of Humenansky's have now sued her. (In two of these suits she was also accused of having sexual relations with her patients, an allegation she denied.) All nine suits were settled out of court. In 1996 Humenansky's license to practice medicine in the state of Minnesota was suspended indefinitely by the Board of Medical Practice. The report ordering the suspension cites a letter Humenansky wrote in her defense: "With respect to the numerous complaints and civil lawsuits against her, Respondent blamed those on the 'perpetrators of childhood sexual assault.'"

Humenansky is not the only one whose MPD practice has had legal ramifications. Braun has now been sued by eleven former patients, including Patricia Burgus and Mary Shanley. Shanley's suit was settled for an undisclosed amount; the Burgus family suit, for a spectacular $10.6 million—which, according to Zachary Bravos, Burgus's (and Shanley's) attorney, is the highest settlement, to date, in a recovered memory case. A hearing to determine whether Braun's medical license should be suspended will be held in 1999. Braun has denied any wrongdoing in the suits against him. (He called the Burgus settlement a "travesty.") Likewise, Dr. Elva Poznanski, who treated the Burgus boys at Rush-Presbyterian and was Braun's codefendant in the Burgus suit (her license too is being reviewed), issued a statement saying, "On the basis of the knowledge available at that time, I would not change the treatment of these boys."[17] As for Rush-Presbyterian, which was also a codefendant in the Burgus suit, again there have been no confessions of wrongdoing. Braun had published his theories on cult abuse before he set up his DD unit at Rush, and Jan Fawcett, Rush's director of psychiatry, had read some of Braun's writings on the subject. Asked on the NBC's "Devil's Advocate" why, under those circumstances, the hospital had permitted Braun to open a treatment center for highly disturbed patients, Fawcett replied, "Just because he had certain ideas that I thought should be checked out doesn't mean he shouldn't start a unit." Such reasoning notwithstanding, Rush-Presbyterian has now closed Braun's DD unit.

But Braun is far from the only one. A malpractice suit was recently filed against D. Corydon Hammond as well. Judith Peterson has been hit with lawsuits by at least eight former patients. Roberta Sachs was one of the codefendants in the Shanley suit. Colin Ross, who prescribed the megadoses of benzodiazepines, is facing litigation in both the United States and Canada. Among the allegations against him in the U.S. suit are negligence, fraud, and conspiracy to commit fraud.

Those are only the civil suits. The criminal trials have now begun, insurance fraud being the primary issue. In 1998 a St. Louis court sentenced recovered-memory therapist Geraldine Lamb to thirty months in prison for making false insurance claims in the case of a patient who, having come to her for help with depression, eventually "remembered" having sacrificed babies as part of a cult operating out of secret caves in southern Illinois. In a more spectacular case, the prime movers of the DD unit at Spring Shadows Glen, where Mary Shanley completed her MPD treatment, went on trial in Houston in 1998. Judith Peterson, together with therapist Sylvia Davis and former hospital administrator George Jerry Mueck, plus psychiatrists Richard Seward and Gloria Keraga (Keraga had already lost a malpractice suit, with the jury awarding $5.8 million to one of her former patients), faced a sixty-count indictment charging that they induced false cult memories, exaggerated diagnoses, coerced staff, and manipulated patient insurance in order to collect millions of dollars' worth of fraudulent claims. This case ended in a mistrial, but in the press coverage of the five months' proceedings, the people of Houston found out a great deal about MPD therapy.

24

Again, this is only a sample. There have been many, many legal cases against therapists in the last five years, and overwhelmingly the therapists are losing. Clinicians across the country are watching the trend, but not more closely than their insurance companies. Until recently, there was a standard clause in psychotherapy malpractice insurance policies saying that coverage would be void under certain conditions—for example, if the therapist was convicted of a felony or had sexual relations with patients. Now, a number of insurers have added a further disqualifying condition: if the therapist uses hypnosis to help patients recover memories of childhood abuse. If only for financial reasons, one of the most disgraceful episodes in the history of psychotherapy seems to be coming to an end. "In but a few years," writes Paul McHugh, the director of psychiatry at Johns Hopkins, "we will all look back" on the MPD movement "and be dumbfounded by the gullibility of the public in the late twentieth century and by the power of psychiatric assertions to dissolve common sense."[18]

If Elizabeth Carlson didn't have multiple personality disorder, has anyone ever had it? That depends on what one means by having it. Every culture contains what medical anthropologists call its "idiom of distress"; in distress, people use their idiom. In south and east Asia, there is a serious disorder, koro, in which the man imagines, with terrible dread, that his penis is being retracted into his body. (There is a female version too.) Koro is almost unheard of in the United States, as anorexia nervosa, said to afflict .5 to 1 percent of young American women, is virtually unknown in societies where people have koro. Mental disorders also go in and out of vogue. In late eighteenth- and early nineteenth-century Europe, there was a fashion for somnambulism, or sleepwalking. (Hence Bellini's *La Sonnambula*.) According to Henri Ellenberger's history of dynamic psychiatry, *The Discovery of the Unconscious*, the somnambulists were said to have otherworldly powers: in their trances, they "would write, swim rivers, or walk over rooftops in full-moon nights."[1] Today somnambulism is considered a minor and transient sleep disorder, usually confined to children, who in most cases will do something quite unremarkable, such as eat a sandwich or go to the bathroom, before returning to bed.

Like psychologically normal people, the psychologically disturbed are hard to slot. Indeed, most psychiatric patients are *comorbid:* they fit the diagnostic criteria for more than one disorder. MPs are an excellent example. According to one authority, the average MPD patient meets the criteria for three to four other psychological disorders—another expert says ten[2]—besides MPD, typical accompaniments including depression, antisocial personality disorder, and borderline personality disorder. This fact, among others, has led many experts to question the *validity* of MPD—the extent to which the term describes a significant pattern of psychological disturbance.[3]

Actually, most American psychiatrists do seem to believe that multiple personality disorder is real but that it rarely occurs spontaneously, without propmting, and therefore does not deserve to be a primary-level diagnosis. Why, they ask, when a diagnostician is faced with a patient who qualifies for numerous different diagnoses, would the choice fall upon this historically rare condition, MPD? That question will occupy most of the remainder of this book, but for now it can be said that a "polyfragmented" multiple with 335 personality states, including a squadron that flies over the hospital by means of astral projection—this was one of Colin Ross's patients[4]—is, for many therapists, a more interesting companion for three hours a week than a woman who passes bad checks and beats her children (antisocial personality disorder) or one who always feels tired, sad, and guilty and doesn't know why (depression).

So the "social construction" of mental illness—the fact that the forms mental illness takes (indeed, the very notion that there is such a thing as mental illness) are the product of shifting cultural assumptions—must be taken into account to explain the rise of MPD. But once acknowledged, the idea can be laid aside. At least in its contemporary, hyper-relativist incarnation, it is foreign to this subject. MPD is a field of angry people, making absolute judgments. They believe that things are real or not real. According to MPD believers, the disorder exists, and not to diagnose it is negligence, even malpractice. According to MPD skeptics, the disorder is over-whelmingly iatrogenic, that is, created by therapy.

≫≪

Both sides, however, agree as to where MPD came from: that it is part of the history of hysteria. Hysteria is the appearance of physical symptoms (typically, convulsions, paralyses, strangulation, breathing problems, numbness, pain) or psychological symptoms (anxiety, emotional outbursts, "spells")—or both—in the absence of any evident organic cause. This is the crux of the disorder: the patient is sick and the doctor doesn't know why. ("Mysteria," one nineteenth-century specialist called it.) The other critical fact about hysteria is that it has almost always been viewed as a woman's disorder. The French internist Paul Briquet, in his 1859 *Treatise on Hysteria*, stated the male-female ratio as one to twenty.[5]

The history of hysteria can be traced back four thousand years, to ancient Egypt. The disorder was also discussed by Hippocrates in the fifth century B.C. Ancient physicians did think, however, that they knew the cause: these strange female symptoms were due to the wandering upward of the uterus, which at that time was considered capable of floating around in the female body. (Hence hysteria's name, from *hystera*, the Greek word for uterus.) Various remedies were proposed, above all marriage, so that the uterus, summoned to do its job, would return to its proper location.

With the rise of Christianity, organic theories of hysteria, as of so much else, were replaced by supernatural explanations: odd female complaints were the work of the devil. Some of the women burned as witches during the sixteenth and seventeenth centuries were probably hysterics, and it is to seventeenth-century doctors protesting these persecutions that we owe the return to an organic theory of hysteria. For the next two centuries physicians debated which organs were at fault. Many reverted to the uterine theory; others, with the rise of neurology, claimed that the problem lay with the nerves.

In the late nineteenth century, the nerve theory culminated in the work of Jean Martin Charcot (1825–1893), a celebrated French neurologist who, in the 1870s, turned his attention to hysteria. Charcot believed that hysteria was a disorder of the central nervous system, though it might be triggered by emotional trauma. He published over a hundred case histories on the subject, and at his hospital in Paris, La Salpetrière (soon heavily populated with hysterics), he gave famous lecture-demonstrations in which his patients, under hypnosis, would undergo hysterical seizures in front of fascinated audiences consisting not only of doctors but journalists, artists, writers, and the general public. These demonstrations were drawn, painted, written about in the popular press. But Charcot was not hysteria's only publicist. No disorder was more important to late nineteenth-century psychiatry. Great doctors devoted their careers to hysteria. Bookstores sold collections of photographs of hysterics in mid-attack. The number of patients multiplied year by year. It was an epidemic, like MPD in the 1980s.

Today, even the most historically sophisticated reader must find it strange that nobody ever wondered whether hysteria might be the result of women's position in society. "From the start," writes G. S. Rousseau in his 1993 essay on the disorder, ". . . it was the public language embodying the female's plight."[6] This possibility seems to have occurred to no one. Yet the physicians of the past viewed hysteria as meaning almost everything else about women. To begin with, there was the idea, implicit in the uterine theory, that whatever was wrong with a woman was due to her sex. Imagine if a man's unexplained medical problems were invariably said to originate in his penis. Yet again and again, any mysterious symptom suffered by a woman was thought to issue from her reproductive anatomy. As it happened, men in former centuries did, like women, have unexplained symptoms, but with rare exceptions, doctors were reluctant to call this male condition hysteria. Instead, it was given another name: hypochondria, melancholy, neurasthenia, spleen. As one

French doctor put it, "A man cannot be hysterical; he has no uterus."[7]

The woman's symptoms were attributed not only to her sex, but to sex. In the ancient theory, hysteria was attributed to sexual deprivation—virginity, widowhood. When the uterine theory was revived after the Renaissance, it took a new turn: the cause of hysteria was woman's outsized sexual appetite, her *furor uterinus*. That was why women chose hysteria, because the treatment was like sex: they would be touched, petted, probed. In some cases, the treatment *was* sex. The electromechanical vibrator was no sooner invented in the 1880s than it was used to treat hysteria. The woman went to the doctor, and he gave her an orgasm.[8]

Conversely, expressions of female sexuality were regarded as hysterical. Mark Micale, in his 1995 book *Approaching Hysteria*, analyzes Emma Bovary, Flaubert's adulteress, as a portrait of hysteria: "dizziness, weak spells, heart palpitations, and bouts of nerves"[9]— convulsions too. Anna Karenina, Tolstoy's adulteress, also qualifies. From women's sexuality it was not far to go to women's moral weakness—their natural deceitfulness, their immaturity—as a further source of hysteria. The link between women and hysteria thus became a tautology. Women developed hysteria not because of some external factor, such as the apportionment of power in society, but simply because they were women. "As a general rule, all women are hysterical," wrote the French physician Auguste Fabre in 1883. "Hysteria, before being an illness, is a temperament, and what constitutes the temperament of women is rudimentary hysteria."[10]

There is a famous painting (1887) by André Brouillet of one of Charcot's lecture demonstrations. In it the great doctor addresses his all-male audience while supporting the swooning body of his star patient, Blanche Wittmann, known at La Salpetrière as *la reine des hystériques*, the queen of the hysterics. The bosom of this attractive young woman is bared almost to the nipples. She is having a hysterical seizure, though if you didn't know this, you might think she had just had an orgasm. Close by stands a bed, site of sleep, illness, sex. Hysteria, before being an illness, was a theory of women.

Some writers, such as Lisa Tickner and Elaine Showalter, have argued that the hysteria craze was an effort to shore up that theory.[11] Many circumstances in the late nineteenth century contributed to the growth of hysteria, but a critical cause was probably the rise of feminism. Organic theories of hysteria, with their stress on women's built-in, constitutional weakness, offered a good argument against women's rights. At the same time, uncooperative, angry women, demanding things like the right to vote, could be labeled hysterical, and they routinely were, both in the medical literature and in the popular press.

※ ※

Out of this concatenation of sex and science was born the study of multiple personality disorder, as a subtype of hysteria. Not all theories of hysteria were organic. Already in the seventeenth century it had been proposed that the phantom illness might be produced by psychological trauma. And increasingly, in the eighteenth and nineteenth centuries, scientists were confronted with evidence that the mind might have some unknown part that influenced behavior, including hysterical behavior. For one thing, there were the somnambulists, who seemed, in their trances, to enter an otherwise closed chamber of the mind.

But the crucial development was the discovery of hypnosis by the Viennese physician Franz Anton Mesmer (1734–1815) in the 1770s. Using a routine that today sounds less like a medical procedure than like a magic show—dim lights, music, cape-waving, the moving about of metal rods in a vat of fluid—Mesmer found that he could cure hysterics. Actually, Mesmer didn't invent hypnosis; shamans had probably been using it since the Stone Age. What he did was bring it to the attention of the medical profession. Furthermore, he didn't know it was hypnosis. He thought he was conducting a physical therapy, adjusting magnetic fluids in his patients' bodies. This notion was eventually discredited, and Mesmer disgraced, but the true meaning of his therapy—that hysteria could be cured by appealing, via suggestion, to another side of consciousness and therefore might originate in the same place—was not lost on others. A number of physicians began experimenting with hypnosis, which they saw as a species of induced somnambulism.

Very gradually over the course of the nineteenth century, there were reports of a bizarre variation on somnambulism, in which the patient went back and forth between two wholly different states of consciousness, often for long periods. The first detailed medical report of what was then called "double consciousness" was published in 1816. Others trickled into print over the next few decades. Then, from the 1870s to the end of the nineteenth century—that is, at the same time as the hysteria outbreak—there was a small rash of such cases. Usually the patient had only two personalities, with at least one-way amnesia and often with the good–bad split. (In a German case reported in 1828, a mild-mannered fellow named Sörgel chopped up a local woodcutter and drank his blood.[12]) Double consciousness locked in with the study of hypnosis and also with the late nineteenth-century vogue for spiritualism, and like those other two factors, it fed and was fed by the romantic cult of the irrational. A literature of the double was born. Robert Louis Stevenson's 1886 *The Strange Case of Dr. Jekyll and Mr. Hyde* is the best-known example, but Heinrich von Kleist, E.T.A. Hoffmann, Poe, and Dostoevsky, together with scores of lesser writers, also contributed to the genre. George du Maurier's 1894 novel *Trilby*, about an artist's model whose hypnotically induced double becomes a world-famous opera singer, was an international best-seller.

These phenomena—hypnosis, hysteria, double consciousness—led to the discovery of the unconscious mind. In the words of a famous book of the period, Max Dessoir's *The Double Ego* (1890), the mind had an "upper consciousness" and a "lower consciousness." The lower consciousness spoke to us in dreams; in hypnosis it was called forth; in double consciousness it emerged spontaneously. As for the cause of double consciousness, the leading theory was that of another physician at La Salpetrière, Pierre Janet (1859–1947), a reserved and fastidious man (the very opposite of the showman Charcot) who raised plants, wrote philosophical treatises, and spent long hours taking case histories from his patients. Double consciousness, said Janet, was caused by childhood trauma. To cope with the trauma, the mind walled it off from awareness—a process Janet called *désagrégation* (later translated as "dissociation"). But the trauma memory remained in the mind, narrowing the person's sphere of action and constantly threatening to invade awareness. In double consciousness and also in hysteria (Janet too saw double consciousness as a form of hysteria), that is what happened: the banished part knocked down the wall and took over. The cure was catharsis. The trauma had to be unearthed and discharged, usually via hypnosis.

If any of this sounds familiar, one of the revelations of Ellenberger's *Discovery of the Unconscious*, the book that revived Janet's reputation, is the extent to which what we think of as Freudian theory was discovered before Freud. But Janet's explanation of double consciousness is not just the germ of Freud's theory; it *is* modern MPD theory, with only a few additions from *Sybil*. Ellenberger's book was published in 1970; *Sybil*, three years later. When the two met—in the context of other circumstances, as we shall see—the modern MPD movement was born.

≫ ≪

Double consciousness was a subject of interest to European psychiatry from about 1880 to the end of the century. Then its headquarters moved to the United States, where the theory was expanded upon, notably by Morton Prince, one of the founders of American experimental psychology and the therapist of another famous multiple, "Miss Beauchamp." But by about 1920, the subject had faded from sight.

It can be said that nineteenth-century MPD died a natural death. Even in its period of greatest vogue, it was still an exotically rare disorder. (The two doctors most interested in it, Janet and Prince, reported only four cases apiece.) Furthermore, people were always skeptical about it, saying that the patients were just trying to get attention or escape blame for misdeeds. Janet himself worried that the condition might be an artifact of hypnosis. Near the end of his life, he demoted it to a form of manic-depressive illness.

But the principal reason for the demise of MPD was probably the demise of hysteria. In his 1995 book *Rewriting the Soul*, the Canadian philosopher Ian Hacking argues that MPD, as an idea, is a parasite: to live, it needs a host to feed on. In the nineteenth century, the host was hysteria. But hysteria too seemed suspect to many physicians. Like Janet with MPD, they wondered if it wasn't a product of hypnosis, or even just suggestion. As long as Charcot lived, his reputation was strong enough to uphold that of hysteria. But after his death in 1893, the diagnosis rapidly died out in France, and people came to ridicule the thing that had once enthralled them. A French neurologist of the early twentieth century reported that when he was a resident at La Salpetrière in 1899, some of the great man's old patients were still there and that if you gave them a small tip, they would produce for you a full-fledged hysterical attack, just as they had for Dr. Charcot.[13]

According to modern MPD believers, however, nineteenth-century MPD didn't die naturally—it was killed, by the man who was to be the lawgiver of modern psychiatry. As noted, much of Freud's theory was based on Janet, together with other navigators of the nineteenth-century unconscious. As his ideas developed, speeded perhaps by an irritated sense of indebtedness, Freud put a distance between himself and his predecessors. He abandoned hypnosis, which was essential to the study of dissociation. Indeed, he rejected dissociation, the idea that discomforting memories could be walled off, remaining pristine in the mind, and he substituted repression, in which the memory, though excluded from consciousness, was continually worked on by the mind. So, fundamentally, he threw out the basic principles of Janet's conceptualization of MPD.

But that is not all. In his seduction theory—his belief, during the 1890s, that his patients' hysterias were due to their having been sexually molested as children—Freud, according to modern MPD theorists, discovered the mother lode, the true cause of multiple personality disorder, the thing that even Janet had not been able to see. And then he walked away from it. As has been argued by a number of writers, Freud had good reasons for giving up his seduction theory: he realized that he had bullied his patients into these "confessions" of childhood abuse; he saw that, under the seduction theory, they were not getting better.[14] So he switched theories, from actual seduction to fantasized seduction—in other words, childhood sexuality—and psychoanalysis was born. But according to MPD theorists, he was right the first time, and he abandoned his position only out of cowardice, because he was afraid of shocking the Viennese medical establishment. He never diagnosed MPD, and his followers sneered at it: Ernest Jones said that "most, perhaps all" MPD cases were fakes.[15] As a result, according to MPD adherents, multiple personality disorder, having only just been discovered, was thrust back into darkness for almost a century more.

There are other factors that contributed to the demise of the MPD diagnosis. One was Swiss psychiatrist Eugen Bleuler's 1911 treatise on "dementia praecox," a condition that Bleuler renamed "schizophrenia" and discussed so compellingly that it became the leading twentieth-century conceptualization of psychosis, absorbing, in the MPD believers' view, many cases that were actually MPD. But according to the MPD establishment, Bleuler is a secondary matter; Freud was the villain. In the words of Colin Ross, "Freud did to the unconscious mind, with his theories, what New York City does to the ocean with its garbage."[16]

3

The Epidemic

The return of multiple personality disorder in the 1970s began with the coming together of two forces, the child protection movement and feminism. In 1962, in the *Journal of the American Medical Association*, a group of Denver pediatricians headed by C. Henry Kempe published an article, "The Battered Child Syndrome," demonstrating via X-rays that very small children—infants, toddlers—had been beaten, presumably by their parents, hard enough to break their bones. This fact, it is now said, had been known to pediatricians for years; only Kempe's group had the stomach to publish it. In any case, it created a furor. The popular press bannered the findings. Commissions were set up. A movement got under way, and in 1974 Congress passed the Child Abuse Prevention and Treatment Act, requiring that teachers, social workers, and therapists report suspected abuse. The law offered them immunity for reporting and prison terms for not reporting.

Already by this time, however, the child protection movement had been joined by feminists, and they gave it a new twist. To Kempe's group, the problem was that children were being physically assaulted. To the feminists, the problem was that female children were being sexually assaulted. Furthermore, as the feminists saw it, this was not something that the society actually disapproved of. On the contrary, it was part of normal female socialization. As social worker Florence Rush put it in a paper presented to the New York

Radical Feminist Rape Conference in 1971, sexual abuse was a way of teaching a girl "to accept a subordinate role; to feel guilty, ashamed, and to tolerate, through fear, the power exercised over her by men." Abused girls thus learned to "become the wives and mothers of America."[1] Childhood sexual abuse was simply part of the machinery of a patriarchal society.

Out of this meeting between feminism and the child protection movement came the so-called recovered-memory, or RM, movement. The first premise of the RM movement is that childhood sexual abuse is very common, affecting about one-third of girls. (The definitions used to arrive at this statistic are so broad that it is a wonder the RM advocates got only one-third. *The Courage to Heal* says that if, as a child, you were "subjected to unnecessary medical treatments" or "bathed in a way that felt intrusive to you" or "fondled, kissed, or held in a way that made you feel uncomfortable," that is sexual abuse, just like rape.[2]) The second premise is that many women develop amnesia for their abuse history but at the same time suffer crippling symptoms caused by the buried memory. Third, to relieve the symptoms, the woman must retrieve the memory and, through various techniques, work through it.

If not one-third, then nevertheless large numbers of women—and many men too—were indeed molested as children. One assumes that the RM movement helped some of these people, probably not so much by inducing them to recall forgotten abuse as by reassuring them that the experience they had never forgotten was a relatively common thing, and not their fault. At the same time, the movement appears to have persuaded thousands of women that because their mothers went on bathing them till they were eight or because a drunken relative at a Christmas party grabbed them in the seat of the pants, they were therefore part of a worldwide sisterhood of sex-abuse victims, condemned for the rest of their lives to live out the consequences of the trauma, just like, for example, survivors of the Holocaust. And it was from the latter that the new group took their name; they too called themselves "survivors."

In the past few years the recovered memory movement has been analyzed and condemned in so many books—Eleanor Goldstein and Kevin Farmer's *True Stories of False Memories*, Richard Ofshe and Ethan Watters's *Making Monsters*, Lawrence Wright's *Remembering Satan*, Elizabeth Loftus and Katherine Ketcham's *The Myth of Repressed Memory*, Michael Yapko's *Suggestions of Abuse*, Ian Hacking's *Rewriting the Soul*, Mark Pendergrast's *Victims of Memory*, Frederick Crews's *The Memory Wars*, Nicholas Spanos's *Multiple Identities and False Memories*, Harrison Pope's *Psychology Astray*, August Piper's *Hoax and Reality*[3]—that it seems unnecessary to rehearse its errors one more time. But the movement is far from dead, and it was the main source of the MPD epidemic, so it must be described briefly.

≫ ≪

The movement was spread, primarily, by "recovery manuals"—self-help books that taught the reader how to begin retrieving her abuse memories. Most of the manuals were published in the eighties, including Bass and Davis's *The Courage to Heal* (1988), which immediately leapt to the front of the field, selling three-quarters of a million copies in its first and second editions. The average recovery manual begins with a symptom checklist, including, as signs of buried abuse memories, most of the common ills of humanity. "Do you feel different from other people?" ask Bass and Davis in the first of their several checklists. "Do you find it hard to trust your intuition?" "Do you have trouble feeling motivated?" "Do you feel you have to be perfect?"[4] If so, you may have been abused. If your life is overcontrolled or if it is chaotic, if you're hyperalert or tune things out, if you're not interested in sex or too interested in sex—in other words, if you're just about anything, this again suggests an abuse history. Medical problems—migraine, asthma, arthritis—are further clues. Other checklists include picking your nose and wearing baggy clothes.[5] One researcher has assembled a catalogue of over nine hundred behaviors said by the RM experts to indicate an abuse history.[6] There are very few women who cannot find a portrait of themselves in these supposed symptoms. "I think I checked off every single one," said an RM retractor interviewed on the *Frontline* documentary "Divided Memories." "I was like, bingo! There was sexual abuse. That's what happened to me."

So that's the first step: you have the symptoms. And if you have no recollection of being abused, that doesn't rule you out. "Many women don't have memories," says *The Courage to Heal.* "This doesn't mean they weren't abused." Indeed, if you don't believe that you were abused, that may be a sign that you were abused. In the words of Renee Fredrickson, whose RM manual *Repressed Memories* was published in 1992 (and who five years later paid $175,000 in settlement of a malpractice suit brought against her by a patient who claimed that Fredrickson implanted in her false memories of incest and ritual cult abuse), "The existence of profound disbelief is an indication that the memories are real." If you become distressed at the suggestion that you were molested, that is a further tip-off. If, on the other hand, you suspect it might have happened, that is proof. As *The Courage to Heal* puts it, "If you think you were abused and your life shows the symptoms, then you were."[7] This sentence has become the most notorious in the RM literature.

But how do you retrieve the memory? By this time in the typical recovery manual, it has been suggested that the reader go to a psychotherapist sympathetic to abuse survivors. In the eighties, such therapists were not hard to find, and they did not need prompting from the patient in order to suspect childhood sexual trauma. Many, many clinicians accepted the one-third rule, and felt they could spot unwitting abuse victims within minutes. (In a 1995 survey by Debra Poole and her colleagues of over thirteen hundred doctoral-level clinicians, one-fifth responded that in cases where they suspected unreported sexual abuse, they were *certain* of this, at least half the time, within the first session.) Not only did they spot it, they said it. Therapist Susan Forward, in her book *Betrayal of Innocence,* writes that when she suspects a sexual abuse history, she simply tells the patient, "You know, in my experience a lot of people who are struggling with many of the same problems as you are have often had some really painful things happen to them as kids—maybe they were beaten or molested. And I wonder if anything like that ever happened to you?"[8] Forward says that she has treated over fifteen hundred incest survivors. In how many of these cases did the incest history begin with her suggestion of it?

Suggestion alone usually doesn't do the job. The RM therapist now deploys other techniques. Some of these—"journaling," guided imagery, the interpretation of dreams as abuse memories—have already been described as part of Elizabeth Carlson's therapy with Diane Humenansky, a good student of RM treatment. There are more. One is hypnosis, of course. Another is "art therapy," whereby, for example, big hands mean his big hands coming toward you. There is "body work," usually in the form of massage, in which any pains you discover are "body memories" of abuse. Also popular are writing exercises. In Laura Davis's *The Courage to Heal Workbook*, a spinoff of *The Courage to Heal*, the nonremembering reader is given some blank pages and told, "Write about whatever you can remember that comes closest to sexual abuse—the first time you felt ashamed or humiliated, for instance. . . . Start with what you have. When you utilize that fully, you usually get more." Betsy Petersen, author of the incest-survivor book *Dancing with Daddy*, decided just to write a short story about incest. (It concerned a three-year-old being fingered in her crib by her father: "I lie there with his fingers crawling over me. . . . My flesh is so soft down there . . . Suddenly he groans.") Reading what she had written, Petersen says, she realized that this was what had happened to her.[9]

The RM initiate may still have doubts, however. She must quell them. One way to do this, Fredrickson suggests, is by "saying to yourself three or four times a day for one week, I believe this problem is about my repressed memories of abuse." Another technique is just to tell others your abuse story again and again. That way,

Fredrickson says, you will intuitively know it is real. But for this to work, you must choose your audience carefully. A cardinal principle of the RM movement, as of other cults, is that new members must avoid contact with any potential source of disconfirmation. Your therapist, above all, must believe that you were abused. So must your friends; any who don't should be weeded out. As for your family, here it may be harder to secure a sympathetic hearing, for it is often someone in your family whom you are accusing of having molested you. Even if you speak not to your "perpetrator"—your father, for example—but to your sister instead, she may resist the idea that her father is a child-molester. According to *The Courage to Heal*, however, she owes it to you to lay aside her doubts. In their advice to siblings, Bass and Davis urge your sisters to "validate" your "reality."[10] And if they find themselves feeling upset over your story, they should ask themselves whether they too weren't abused.

The rule, as *The Courage to Heal* states unequivocally, is "Believe the survivor."[11] If your family violates the rule, stop seeing them. And don't worry that you might be accusing them wrongly. "If months or years down the road, you find you are mistaken about details, you can always apologize and set the record straight," says Fredrickson,[12] apparently ignorant of the special nature of the crime involved. (By the time Beth Rutherford of Springfield, Missouri, set the record straight in 1996, her father, a minister, had lost his job, and the family was shattered. Beth, who had claimed that her father had repeatedly raped her and had forced her into two coat-hanger abortions, turned out upon medical examination to be a virgin. The Rutherford family's defamation and malpractice suit against Beth's therapist was settled for $1 million.) But in the padded cell of validation that the survivor is instructed to create around herself, it is unlikely that she will discover any reason to believe she was wrong.

An important adjunct of RM therapy is group therapy. Even women who have no abuse memories are routed into "survivor groups," where they can benefit from "chaining," in which each woman's abuse memory stimulates the emergence of the others'. As

Judith Herman, author or *Trauma and Recovery*, writes approvingly, "The group helps each individual to enlarge her story." MPD and satanic ritual abuse have often been products of such enlargement. In the words of an ex-survivor interviewed by the *Toronto Star* in 1992, "The stories got grosser and grosser. . . . If you didn't have memories, you didn't get any attention." On the other hand, you get a great deal of attention from the group, plus praise for conquering your denial, when you do get memories.[13]

In addition, there are the pleasures of group solidarity, and these extend beyond the individual group. There are newsletters that survivors can subscribe to, hiking clubs they can join, abuse-theme books and tapes—even a board game, "Survivor's Journey"—they can order. They can get a survivor pen pal. (These resources are listed in the back of *The Courage to Heal*.) At the same time, there have been movies for them to see—*Dolores Claiborne* and *A Thousand Acres*, among others—and countless television programs for them to watch. Even more than MPD, incest has been standard fare of recent TV talk shows. The celebrities came forward—Oprah, Roseanne, the rest. Dead celebrities were also corralled. Elvis, we are now told, was molested as a child. In 1996, in the *London Times*, psychiatrist Elinor Kapp gave the opinion that Queen Elizabeth I was also abused, as could be seen from an early portrait of her: "There is . . . a frozen watchfulness that recalls to me countless victims of deprived or abused childhoods."[14]

In short, recovered memory, beginning as a political movement, became a craze, a juggernaut. Judith Herman says that in her survivor groups, "virtually every woman who has defined the goal of recovering memories has been able to do so." Bass and Davis also report a 100 percent success rate: "So far, no one we've talked to thought she might have been abused, and then later discovered she hadn't been. The progression always goes the other way, from suspicions to confirmation."[15] And Bass and Davis, together with their colleagues, have given numerous workshops to train therapists in their foolproof method. What they haven't done in person, their book has done. The Debra Poole group's 1995 survey of thirteen hundred doctoral-level therapists found that almost half had recommended *The Courage to Heal* to their patients. A quarter focused their therapy on childhood abuse and used suggestive techniques such as hypnosis to unearth abuse memories. Using these figures, Mark Pendergrast, in his *Victims of Memory*, calculates that since 1988 several million people have come to believe that they have recovered memories of childhood sexual abuse. How many of them actually suffered what most people would call sexual abuse?

True or not, many of these accusations have been taken to court, typically in the form of a civil suit with the survivor seeking to recover damages from the alleged abuser. A major spur to such suits was the highly publicized murder trial of George Franklin in California in 1990. In 1969, an eight-year-old girl, Susan Nason, was found murdered in the woods near Foster City, California. The crime was never solved. Then, twenty years later, a woman named Eileen Franklin Lipsker, who had been a friend of Nason's, came forward saying that via a recovered memory she now knew that she had witnessed the crime, that the murderer had raped Susan before killing her, and that he was her father, George Franklin. Lipsker eventually gave five competing versions of how her memory returned; once it was via a "flashback," once through hypnosis, and so on. Furthermore, all the verifiable details in her account had already been published in newspaper articles before she went to the police. Nevertheless, George Franklin was not a man to arouse sympathy. (Whether or not he was a murderer, evidence brought forward at the trial indicated that he had beaten and molested his daughters.) He was convicted.

The conviction was later overturned, but that did not happen until 1995. In the intervening years, the Franklin trial—the first criminal prosecution to be based on recovered memory—gave to RM not just publicity but a new legal respectability. Meanwhile, starting in 1989, state legislatures began extending their statutes of limitations to allow for recovered memory. (By now about half the states give the plaintiff one to six years, not after the crime but after remembering the crime, in which to sue, though courts in different jurisdictions have applied the new statutes in different ways.) The number of recovered memory lawsuits soared. Law firms began leaving packets of information with women's centers. In one, there was a sample letter that began, "Dear Mr. and Mrs. Blank: Your child has retained me to represent her for the sexual and physical assaults perpetrated on her by Mr. Blank when she was a minor. She has suggested that we attempt to settle this matter outside the legal arena. . . . At this time, prior to filing a lawsuit, we are prepared to settle the case to $250,000 "[16]

It was within the machinery of the recovered memory movement that multiple personality disorder was reborn. Not all recoverers of sex abuse memories developed MPD, but almost all MPs had such memories, and many of them first manifested their multiplicity in the course of RM therapy. Their condition was seen as the extreme result of childhood sex abuse trauma, and one that, because the alters concealed the memories, blocked resolution of the trauma. So therapists who had helped their patients recover trauma memories and then found that the patients were not getting better began to look for evidence of MPD. They soon found it.

≫ ≪

Many, many circumstances in the 1970s and 1980s fed into MPD. Some were developments within psychology. Starting in the 1960s, there was a revival of interest in hypnosis, which was to play so large a role in MPD. Then, in the 1970s, as part of a continuing protest against the Vietnam War, a new and (it was hoped) stigma-free diagnostic category, posttraumatic stress disorder, or PTSD, was developed for Vietnam veterans. Fifteen percent of male Vietnam veterans eventually received this diagnosis, which by 1987 yielded a tax-free income of $1,800 per month in the case of full disability.

The psychiatrist Fred Frankel has analyzed the rise of PTSD in Vietnam veterans and the rise of RM in women as part of a single phenomenon:

> Veterans in emotional distress were often helped by being encouraged, in the security of the therapeutic encounter, to revisit traumatic memories. . . . Dreams of combat, although often only resembling what had been experienced or feared, were used as stepping stones to a mental reenactment of combat experience. Women who had experienced domestic violence, childhood sexual abuse, and incest came to be viewed as counterparts of these veterans. By encouraging patients to regard themselves as survivors rather than victims, therapists believed they could help in reestablishing the self-esteem of veterans and of women who felt devalued and degraded by their experiences.

For feminist therapists who believed that all women were fundamentally traumatized (Bonnie Burstow in *Radical Feminist Therapy*: "Faced with any female client, we can assume some degree of childhood abuse"), it was not far to go to extend the same consolation to women who had no abuse memories. In the eyes of some trauma experts, we live in a brutalizing society, and no special proof is required to establish that harm has been done.[17]

This is where psychology meets politics, and politics, together with social change, was probably the foremost cause of the MPD and RM epidemics. A critical contributor was the breakdown of the family. In the 1960s and 1970s, when today's memory-recoverers were children, the national divorce rate nearly tripled. Stepfathers are far more likely than fathers to abuse children, and a father you haven't seen in ten years is easier to accuse than one you have dinner with every Sunday.

With the dissolution of the family came pop psychology, notably the so-called *recovery movement*. This recovery movement, though connected to the recovered-memory movement, makes far broader claims: that 98 percent of families are "dysfunctional" (this is the figure given by John Bradshaw, the movement's leader); that in consequence most of us are plagued with various "addictions" and "codependencies"; that these conditions can be treated by our entering "twelve-step" programs based on Alcoholics Anonymous and, like AA, requiring that we confess our permanent disability. (The recovery movement, like the RM and MPD movements, is disproportionately female.) With its emphasis on the "inner child," the infant part of us that cries out for the satisfaction of needs unmet by our families, the recovery movement probably supplied the child alters for many future MPs.

Another contributor was the rise of New Age. In the late nineteenth century, as noted, there was an enormous vogue for spiritualism—seances were an ordinary social event—and this fueled the interest in hysteria and double consciousness. So it has been in the late twentieth century. From the 1960s to the present there has been a widespread fashion for occult and psychic phenomena: for channeling, for UFO- and Elvis-sightings, for angels and unicorns and crystals. In many American cities there are now "angel groups" where participants get together with a facilitator who puts them into a state where they can make contact with their "angels." In some cases, the angel, guiding the hand of his or her protégé, will spirit-write a message. This is roughly the same process by which alters invade a "host" personality. In general, New Age, with its vision of a world teeming with unseen presences, and with its anti-scientific bias, meshed neatly with the rise of multiple personality disorder. Many MPs reported paranormal experiences: "mental telepathy, telekinesis, clairvoyance, possession, contact with ghosts or poltergeists, and knowledge of past lives," to quote one group of researchers.[18] As noted, a patient described by Colin Ross had alters that flew over the hospital by means of astral projection.

Nor is belief in such things confined to the patients. Ross, in his MPD casebook, expresses his regret that ESP has been "suppressed by the intelligentsia." Likewise the study of demons. "Why, scientifically, should demons not exist?" he asks. Once, he reports, he had a patient who claimed that she had been impregnated by aliens. He expressed doubt over her story, he says, but that was "before I had heard about the current epidemic of UFO abductions." Now he has learned not to express doubt. This patient, he writes, "taught me that there is a connection of some kind between UFO abductions and the use of women as breeders for Satanic cults."[19] Thus has New Age fed RM, MPD, and satanic ritual abuse claims.

These new philosophies, meanwhile, were accompanied in the media by what was probably the most exuberant outbreak of prurience and violence since the late Roman empire. The electronic entertainment industry was unquestionably the main source of imagery for the newly recovered memories, and the cause of the therapists' credulity in the face of those memories. With the "Freddy" movies around, with rap singers singing about butchering women, with video games making a sport of tearing people's entrails out, what is a little afterbirth-eating? The media supplied alters too. MPD patients have reported Madonna alters, Mr. Spock alters, Ninja Turtle alters. The very form of the disorder, with its "switching," bears a striking resemblance to that of our fast-cutting visual entertainments. Ian Hacking notes that MPD came in right around the time people acquired remote control for their television sets. The multiples were channel-surfing. Pointing to another likely source, George Ganaway has remarked on the resemblance between MPD therapy and video games: as soon as one layer of alters has been identified and its dark deeds reenacted, another layer would descend, and another, until, as Ganaway put it, "the therapist finally tires of the game or the host personality runs out of quarters."[20]

The Internet has done its part too, at least as a source of information—or contamination. There are Web sites for multiples, Web sites for ritual abuse claimants. By clicking on, suggestible people can find out what curious signs led others to the discovery of their MPD or their cult history and begin looking for such signs in their own lives. It has been proposed, furthermore, that by inviting its users to leave their messages in the guise of created "personae," the Internet in a way encourages experimentation with multiplicity. In the words of sociologist–psychologist Sherry Turkle:

> When people adopt an online persona they cross a boundary into highly-charged territory. Some feel an uncomfortable sense of fragmentation, others a sense of relief. Some detect the possibilities for self-discovery, even self-transformation. A 26-year-old graduate student in history says: "When I join a new virtual community and I create a character and know I have to start typing my description, I always feel a sense of panic. Like I could find out something I don't want to know."

Turkle is not claiming that the Internet causes MPD—only that, in her words, "MPD exists in a cultural force field that is increasingly open to considerations of multiplicity."[21]

It can be said, in general, that the phenomenal expansion and refinement of media technology in the past few decades helped lay the foundation of unreality on which the RM/MPD movement grew. One of the most surprising revelations of the RM/MPD case histories is that many people no longer trust their memories of what they have and haven't done in their lives. Recall the story of Paul Ingram, subject of Lawrence Wright's *Remembering Satan*. Ingram was a fundamentalist Christian, a county sheriff, and head of the Republican party in his town. Yet when asked if he had had homosexual relations with his poker buddy Jim Rabie, or worn his wife's underwear, he merely answered, "I don't think so." Rabie, when arrested as an accomplice in Ingram's alleged assaults on his daughters, also didn't know whether or not he was guilty. He had no memory of molesting the Ingram girls, but this didn't mean to him that he hadn't done so. "Give me the responsibility, because I've blocked it out enough," he said. "If I can't remember this, then I am so damn dangerous I do not deserve to be loose."[22] There turned out to be no evidence against him, yet by the time the charges were dropped, he had spent five months in jail. As for Ingram, he was convicted, on charges that may be wholly groundless. He is still in prison, serving a twenty-year sentence.

In this and other RM cases, religious fundamentalism, with its dramatic notions of sin and penitence, clearly played a major role. Another factor was popular psychology. (Ingram and Rabie were repeatedly grilled by alleged experts who told them that they could "block out" all memory of having subjected the Ingram children to violent abuse.) But given those two forces, it seems likely that the entertainment industry also plays its part. Daily, hourly—the average American watches more than four hours of television per day—we are exposed to illusory representations far more vivid than our own lives. It is not surprising that some people come to confuse true and false. Finally, popular entertainment has probably contributed to the peculiar *tone* of the RM/MPD movement, its combination of luridness and righteousness. Michael Jackson fondling his genitals on stage and singing "Heal the World": this is the same strange land from which we get the RM/MPD experts retailing sex stories under the aegis of child protection.[23]

But greater than all these causes, and feeding on them, were the "culture wars" of the 1980s and 1990s. Strange to say, combatants on both sides embraced MPD and RM. To many leftists, these traumatic conditions were simply further demonstrations of the victimization of the populace in general by a small, historically privileged group of white males. To many conservatives, RM and MPD were results of the new permissiveness that was tearing society apart: sexual freedom, divorce, women going to work and leaving their children with strangers. A major force on the right was a factor just mentioned, evangelical Christianity, which has grown at a phenomenal rate in the last twenty years and, in the process, has entered the field of psychotherapy. (From 1991 to 1996, membership in the American Association of Christian Counselors increased from seven hundred to seventeen thousand.) "Christian counselors," often without any advanced training in psychology, have been involved in a number of the most scandalous MPD cases (including the Beth Rutherford case), and many MPs come from strict Christian backgrounds.

Apart from Christian fundamentalism, the one force most closely tied with the RM and MPD movements is feminism. As noted, it was from the conjunction of feminism with the child protection movement that RM therapy grew. On the cover of one of the most outrageous RM manuals, E. Sue Blume's *Secret Survivors*, is a blurb by Gloria Steinem: this book, Steinem says, "can set millions free." Steinem has also been an MPD activist. In 1993 she conceived and narrated an HBO TV show, "Multiple Personalities: The Search for Deadly Memories," in which, for example, an MP named Gretchen, with the cameraman conveniently handy, opens her "journal" and finds its pages smeared with dried blood. In her best-selling book *Revolution from Within* Steinem actually sings the praises of MPD, as a source of hidden potential: "People in different alters can . . . perfect a musical or linguistic talent that is concealed to the host personality, have two or even three menstrual cycles in the same body, and handle social and physical tasks of which they literally do not think themselves capable."[24] In her acknowledgments, Steinem thanks Bennett Braun for his help with *Revolution from Within*. In 1992, when the book was published, Braun's MPD patient Mary Shanley lay in a drug stupor in Houston while Judith Peterson—whom Steinem thanks, along with Braun, for help with the HBO show—interrogated Shanley as to her cult alters' satanic projects. Apart from pornography, the RM/MPD movement is probably the only cause that has been capable of uniting the feminists with the right-wing fundamentalists, a fact that should have given the feminists pause.

≫ ≪

With these committed supporters, and with a large middle ground of therapists willing to believe, MPD grew year by year. If Colin

Ross's calculations are correct, tens of thousands of people received the diagnosis in the eighties and nineties, and according to some experts, this was far fewer than should have received it. Ross estimated that the prevalence of MPD in the general population was 1 percent (as high as schizophrenia), which meant that millions of additional MPs were walking around undiagnosed. He and his colleagues set about training therapists to spot them. A Canadian therapist, Margo Rivera, leads workshops for that purpose. In 1992 she reported that twenty-five hundred professionals had taken her course. A 1993 CBC documentary, "Mistaken Identities," produced by Michelle Métivier, followed the career of one of Rivera's students, Dale Ault, a social worker based in a small town, Parry Sound, north of Toronto. After Ault learned from Rivera's workshop how to spot and treat MPD, Parry Sound suffered an outbreak of the disorder—fifteen cases, several of them eventually suicidal. Ault has since moved on; reportedly, he now practices in the United States. (In 1997 a malpractice suit brought against him by four of his Parry Sound patients was settled for an undisclosed amount.) On the CBC program, Alan Seltzer, the therapist who succeeded Ault at Parry Sound's mental health center, says, "I can't treat these people for their presenting problems now. I'm . . . treating them for the result of the therapy. It's a whole new disorder in a sense." Rivera, in her training manual, writes that she wants to open her course to nontherapists as well: teachers, clergy, people who work in women's centers.[25]

As the scope of the disorder grew, so did its viability in the courts. Multiples were among the plaintiffs in the RM lawsuits; in other legal proceedings, MPD was invoked for purposes of criminal prosecution, as recovered memory was in the George Franklin case. In a 1990 Wisconsin rape trial, the accuser claimed that although she had accepted the defendant's sexual invitation, it was not she who consented, but one of her forty-six alters. She had MPD, she said, and the defendant knew it. Six of her alters eventually testified, and the one who had consented was found: "Jennifer." The defendant was convicted of second-degree assault.[26]

None of this seemed strange to the MPD community. On the contrary, such acceptance seemed to them just the beginning of what would be a thorough revision of our understanding of mental illness, based on MPD. MPD, Colin Ross wrote, was the most important disorder in psychiatry, one that had taught him that "virtually all symptoms in psychiatry are potentially trauma-driven and dissociative in nature"—in other words, variants of MPD. He prophesied that this truth, once understood, would create a wholesale "paradigm shift" in psychiatry. The two dominant models, the biomedical and the psychoanalytic, would be laid aside, and the trauma model would take their place. Ross was not alone in predicting a great destiny for MPD. Frank Putnam, in his textbook on the disorder, wrote that in the future MPD would be seen as "the centerpiece for models of human consciousness."[27]

To others, however, MPD was not a revolution but a fad. From the very beginning, people wondered about the sudden rise of the disorder and its curiously narrow distribution, the fact that the overwhelming majority of patients were white, female, and North American. The predominance of women could perhaps be explained. In many psychological disorders, one sex greatly outnumbers the other. Furthermore, girls are more vulnerable than boys to sexual assault. But what about the scarcity of blacks? According to a 1994 report by the U.S. Department of Health and Human Services, the rate of child maltreatment for blacks is more than double what it is for whites, and black women writers have repeatedly claimed that sexual abuse is a major problem for black girls. (Think of Alice Walker's *The Color Purple* or Maya Angelou's *I Know Why the Caged Bird Sings*.) So if childhood trauma was the cause of MPD, where were the black MPs?

More than that, why was the disorder centered in North America? For all its problems, North America is one of the least trauma-ridden areas in the world today. Responding to Colin Ross's MPD prevalence estimate of 1 percent, based on a survey of households in Winnipeg, the South African psychiatrist Michael Simpson asked, "Why, in peaceful Winnipeg (where one recalls no major wars, famines, or disasters, and the incidence of child abuse is surely no higher than in other comparable communities) does Ross find so many cases . . . while we in Africa haven't yet been able to find a case?" And why, especially in the beginning, did so many of the MPs seem to come out of the offices of so few therapists, the very ones who were publicizing this syndrome? Why, indeed, did these therapists seem to leave epidemics of MPD in their wake? In 1992 Donald Ross, the residency training director at Sheppard Pratt Health System in Baltimore, reported that the number of MPD diagnoses at Sheppard Pratt increased 900 percent in the two years after an MPD expert joined the hospital's staff.[28]

To all concerned, it was clear that the appearance of MPD had something to do with therapy. The reason the new multiples were overwhelmingly white, female, and North American is that that, overwhelmingly, is the group that goes for psychotherapy: white women in North America. And the reason that these patients were coming out of the offices of certain psychotherapists is that those therapists were the ones diagnosing the disorder. The MPD experts did not deny this fact—they were proud of it. To them it meant that while the world was teeming with undiagnosed MPD, only they knew enough to recognize it. To MPD skeptics, it meant something else: that MPD was being *created* by therapy. Psychiatrist John Hochman went so far as to suggest that MPD be moved, in *DSM*, to the appendix on "culture bound syndromes": "Just as some exotic syndromes are confined to Japan, or certain South Sea Islands, [MPD] is a syndrome geographically related to high concentration zones of therapists who identify with the beliefs of a particular psychological subculture."[29]

Among the early critics of the MPD movement were Corbett H. Thigpen and Hervey M. Cleckley, the therapist–authors of *The*

Three Faces of Eve. In 1984, Thigpen and Cleckley wrote an article claiming that the recent rise of MPD was due simply to misdiagnosis. Since the publication of *Eve* nearly three decades earlier, they said, hundreds of "multiples" had been sent to them by therapists for confirmation of the diagnosis. Other patients came on their own: "We have had long-distance telephone calls from persons announcing themselves as multiple personalities—one went so far as to have each of her personalities introduce itself and speak in a different voice. Similarly, we have had photographs sent to us of the different personalities . . . and one woman changed handwriting styles from paragraph to paragraph in letters to us."[30] In all these cases, they claimed, they had found exactly one true MPD. In their view the MPD epidemic was just a fashion, created by gullible therapists.

This article probably had less effect than it should have. The epidemic was already in full swing. Furthermore, Eve's therapists were not hard to brush off. Eve was the *ancien régime* of MPD—only three alters, no sex abuse history. Actually, her case was a little more complicated than that. In 1975, shortly after the publication of *Sybil*, a Virginia housewife named Chris Sizemore came forward and announced that she was Eve. Apparently, Sizemore did not intend to stand by as Sybil became the world's most famous MP. She had had twenty-one personalities (five more than Sybil), she now announced. She went on television, she gave lectures, she wrote books. But to Sizemore's credit, she never developed a history of childhood sexual abuse, the thing that would have ensured her acceptance by the post-Sybil MPD field. As a result—and probably also because her therapists tried to rain on the MPD parade—other MPs, at conferences, sometimes accuse her of being "in denial." The experts aren't fond of her story either. According to Frank Putnam's MPD textbook, *The Three Faces of Eve* gave "a misleading picture of MPD and ironically may have helped to obscure the clinical features of the disorder."[31] Eve, then, was born too soon. Not she but Sybil became the picture of MPD.

Eventually, however, Sybil's case too came under attack by a man who had treated her. Sybil was highly dependent on her therapist, Cornelia Wilbur. Also, she was suicidal. So when Wilbur went on vacation, she assigned Sybil to a back-up therapist, the psychoanalyst Herbert Spiegel. One day, says Spiegel, he was having a session with Sybil and he asked her a question: "And Sybil said, 'Well, do you want me to be Helen?' I said, 'Why would you think I would want that?' She said, 'Well, when I talk to Dr. Wilbur, when I get to this thing, she wants me to be Helen.' And I said, 'No, you don't have to if you don't want to. I can hear you just as Sybil.' And she said, 'Fine, I'd prefer it that way.' That's when I found out what Connie was doing with this case."[32]

Spiegel is a hypnosis expert. Sybil was extraordinarily hypnotizable. (Indeed, she earned some money by serving as a research subject for Spiegel, and also as demonstration subject in his course on hypnosis at Columbia.) Like many other high-hypnotizables, she was also naturally dissociative; she spontaneously entered self-hypnotic trances. And those trances, as Spiegel explains it, were what Wilbur called Sybil's alters: "When Sybil got into those states, Connie, who was a Freudian-oriented psychoanalyst—knowing little about dissociation, little about hypnosis—made it easier for herself to communicate with them by giving them a name." And the more she addressed them by names separate from Sybil's, the more they became separate from Sybil, all sixteen of them, eventually. "If Connie had known more about hypnosis," Spiegel says, "she wouldn't have coached Sybil to have all these different identities. She would have brought all the parts together right away."

She finally did bring them together, when she had to. By 1965 Sybil's treatment had dragged on for eleven years. Wilbur was leaving New York, moving to Kentucky. Furthermore, she had a journalist, Flora Rheta Schreiber, interested in writing a book on the case, but Schreiber refused to start until the case was closed. So Sybil got fused. "The point I'm making," says Spiegel, "is that you can fuse *any* time. You can fuse even before you bring them apart.

I've had potential multiples, several of them, but they never *became* multiples, because I didn't coach them. They have these transient episodes where they go somewhere else or become something else, and instead of saying, 'Aha! We caught something,' instead of giving them emotional green stamps because 'Oh, you make me feel so good, because we're discovering the real person,' I convey to them that 'You don't have to fragment to talk to me, I can accept you as a total person.' So I bring them together right away, before they glorify their fragments."

Spiegel adds that when Schreiber was in negotiation with a publisher for the book that was to become *Sybil*, she asked him to coauthor the book with her and Wilbur. He was interested. Then she told him that the book was going to be a case history of multiple personality disorder. "I said to her, 'But Sybil wasn't a multiple personality. Those things were artificial fragments, artificially created by Connie. When Sybil was with me, she didn't have to be those people.' And Schreiber said, 'We have to call it a multiple. That's what the publisher wants. That's what will make it sell.' Hysteria wasn't good enough. Dissociative disorder wasn't good enough. It had to be a multiple personality, or the publisher wouldn't take it. I said, 'No, thanks,' and after that, when I saw Connie at conferences, she wouldn't speak to me. She looked the other way. But I didn't think about it much. I had no idea the book was going to set off a revolution." When it did, Spiegel started giving interviews. "Lawsuits are one way to stop this," he says. "A better way would be some professional discipline."

Apart from Spiegel's testimony, there are other troubling things about the case of Sybil Dorsett. It was never written up in the professional literature, where it would have been subjected to scientific standards of reporting. (The MPD experts say that no professional journal would accept it, because the profession didn't accept MPD. Perhaps this is true, though it should be noted that twenty years earlier, in 1954, Thigpen and Cleckley somehow managed to get the *Journal of Abnormal and Social Psychology* to publish a report on Eve.)

Sybil's story was published as a mass-market book, and it reads like one. Indeed, it reads like *Peyton Place*:

> The Dorsetts' next-door neighbor was a recluse, the woman across the street a dwarf, and the man down the street his thirteen-year-old daughter's rapist who, after the event, went right on living in the same house with her as though nothing had happened. It was all part of the curious deformity and lewdness, resulting in assorted illegitimate children, that ran like a subterranean current through this town, outwardly so average, so normal.[33]

Schreiber's description of Sybil's family history runs along the same lines. (One aunt, a psychiatric nurse, ran a "house of assignation for nuns" out of her basement.[34]) Things happen in the book that are scientifically impossible. At one point Sybil, in mid-crisis, hits the ceiling, apparently by abreactive levitation. Elsewhere she remembers events from when she was six months old, even six weeks old, while the rest of us, for neurological reasons, remember almost nothing before age three or four.[35] If these events are fiction, why should the rest of Schreiber's account be taken as fact?

There is also the matter of Sybil's response to Eve. If Eve competed with her famous successor, the compliment was apparently returned. In *Sybil* Schreiber firmly points out that although Thigpen and Cleckley's 1954 report on Eve in the *Journal of Abnormal and Social Psychology* was already in print when Wilbur diagnosed Sybil as a multiple, Wilbur had not read the article. (She had asked for it at the Academy of Medicine library, Schreiber says, but the library didn't have it.) A few chapters earlier, however, Schreiber seems to have forgotten about the Eve problem, for there she reports that Sybil, from the very start of her treatment with Wilbur in October 1954, spent hours in the library reading psychiatric case histories. One of those histories was no doubt Eve's, for it was in

December 1954, only months after the publication of Thigpen and Cleckley's report on this utterly rare disorder, unknown to the general public, that Sybil, in Wilbur's office, came down with the same disorder.

Actually, it is possible that Sybil began her reading of the psychiatric literature *before* she went to Wilbur in 1954, and that Eve's case is what brought her to Wilbur. Sybil had consulted Wilbur nine years earlier, for a few sessions, and at that time there was no talk of multiple personalities. All this is very curious, though it should be added that according to Spiegel, Schreiber's dates are wrong: Wilbur, he says, treated Sybil for years as a schizophrenic before switching to the MPD diagnosis. But whatever the birth date of Sybil's first alter, the chances are very good that this case, which served as the basis for current MPD theory and which, as Putnam approvingly states, provided the "template" for all subsequent cases,[36] was largely manufactured, first in therapy by Wilbur, then in writing by Schreiber, possibly with some help from Sybil.

Wilbur and Schreiber are now dead and cannot defend their claims, but further reason to doubt them was put forth at a 1998 meeting of the American Psychological Association by Robert Rieber, a psychologist at John Jay College of Criminal Justice in New York. Rieber was a friend of Schreiber's, and in 1972, when he was beginning work on a study of the use of language by the mentally ill, Schreiber gave him several tapes of conversations between herself and Wilbur on the subject of Sybil. Rieber eventually abandoned his language study and stored the tapes in his office. Recently, in the wake of the MPD controversy, he went looking for them and found two hours of conversation. These, he says, document not the discovery of an MPD case but the construction of one, via hypnosis, sodium pentothal, and therapeutic suggestion. Wilbur, Rieber says, was eager to have an MPD patient, so she turned Sybil into one: "It is clear from Wilbur's own words that she was not exploring the truth but rather planting the truth as she wanted it to be."

At one point in the conversations, for example, Wilbur tells Schreiber that she had to list for Sybil the names of her "alters" in order to get her to respond in the appropriate voice. "Sybil is a phony multiple-personality case at best," says Rieber.[37]

Around the same time as Rieber's presentation, Sybil was finally identified, by Peter Swales, a historian who has tracked down the true identities of a number of Freud's patients, and Mikkel Borch-Jacobsen, a literature professor at the University of Washington. (The two are now working on a television documentary and also a book on Sybil.) She was Shirley Ardell Mason, from Minnesota, and her connection with Wilbur did not end with the conclusion of her eleven-year therapy. When Wilbur moved to Lexington, Kentucky, so did Mason, to be near the doctor. According to a neighbor, "When Dr. Wilbur wasn't there [at Mason's house], Ms. Mason was at Dr. Wilbur's house." Wilbur died in 1992. (She left Mason $25,000 in her will.) Then Mason died in 1998, at the age of seventy-five. It is a shame that she was not identified early enough to answer questions about her case. According to Rieber, she vacillated on whether or not Schreiber's account was accurate. But if she had been contacted, what could she have told us? The book put together by Wilbur and Schreiber had been her story for years. Furthermore, she received one-third of the book's royalties. (Another third went to Wilbur, another to Schreiber.) Would she have said that it wasn't true?[38]

4

The Therapy

Skepticism about multiple personality disorder must have troubled some people in the field, but others remained undiscouraged, and one can see why. MPD is a highly complex disorder. Scores of alters, often divided into competing families and factions, and with an intricate network of amnesias, alliances, and enmities separating and connecting them: how could this cat's cradle be created by therapeutic suggestion? It seems impossible.

It is not. To explain this, I will rely on the therapy outlined by Frank Putnam in his *Diagnosis and Treatment of Multiple Personality Disorder*. I choose Putnam in the interest of fairness. His book is the most respected in the field—a "classic text," as his colleague Richard Kluft has called it.[1] Also, he is one of the most cautious of the MPD experts. Unlike others, he believes that the disorder is rare; he insists on medical examinations (so that if a patient who claims that she has had two coat-hanger abortions is a virgin, he will know this); he avoids medication and hospitalization; he is not optimistic about MPD's curability; he regards reports of satanic ritual abuse as nonsense.[2] On the evidence of his book, he is humane and humble. When he doesn't know something, he says so. This must be kept in mind as we look at Putnam's therapy: he is the wise-father end of the field.

The other thing that must be understood is the condition of the patient when she arrives for her first session with the therapist. In

reviewing this treatment, the reader will probably think repeatedly, "How can the patient believe this? How can she choose this condition, this life, over a regular life?" But patients who get diagnosed as multiples do not have regular lives, haven't for a long time. On average, they have spent seven years in the mental health system. According to various patient surveys, almost 90 percent of them are depressed, 61 percent have made serious suicide attempts, 57 percent have a history of drug abuse, 20 percent have worked as prostitutes, and 12 percent have criminal records. Their lives, says Putnam, are a "tragic mess,"[3] and they are exactly at the age—late twenties, early thirties—when one asks, "Is this what it's always going to be like for me?"

As for the question of how they could believe what the therapist is saying, recall that most people diagnosed as MPs are highly hypnotizable. As we saw, this doesn't just mean that they can be hypnotized and talked into something or other. It also means that they are probably dissociative—like Sybil, they spontaneously enter hypnoid states, where they become "something else"—and highly suggestible, ready to accept your interpretation of what they are when they are something else. As noted, many report paranormal experiences: ESP, clairvoyance, out of body excursions. If you tell them there are other "parts" hiding inside them, they may be quite willing to believe this.

Finally, most of the women diagnosed as multiples are desperate for a kind relationship. To read MPD case histories—not the extravagant ones, where the girl is nailed to a cross, but the regular ones, where she made dinner for her brother out of a can while her alcoholic father beat up her mother; where, if she was not sexually abused, she was physically abused, left home early, had terrible boyfriends, got pregnant young, didn't know what to do with the child—is very sad. Many of these women have no sense that they can command the love or attention of others. "Their lifelong experience," says Putnam, "is that they drive other people away." When at last they find a person who is genuinely interested in them, that relationship becomes, in the words of MPD authority Richard Kluft, "the most powerful and/or gratifying event of their lives."[4] And if the person's interest in them is based on the belief that they have three hundred personalities, so what? At least he cares.

That is the patient. Here is the therapy, according to Putnam. The woman, when she comes for her first appointment, typically shows no multiplicity, no MPD. The job for the therapist, then, is to "smoke out" the alters. Putnam asks the patient whether she has ever felt like more than one person, and if her reply is encouraging in any way, he then asks, "Do you ever feel as if there is some other part . . . of yourself that comes out and does or says things that you would not do or say?" Again, if her response is even so much as ambiguous, he presses forward, asking, "Can this other part come out and talk with me?"[5]

Often, this yields nothing. "I would urge persistence," Putnam says. The therapist should probe energetically, and at length. A typical diagnostic (that is, smoking-out-the-alters) session lasts about three hours, he writes, "though it may be necessary to spend a large part of the day with some highly secretive MPD patients."[6] If that doesn't work, he uses the old standby, hypnosis. He especially recommends hypnotic age regression, in which the patient is supposedly taken back to childhood. He also recommends ideomotor signaling, whereby, instead of speaking, the patient gives her answers by means of prearranged hand signals, such as raising the index finger to mean yes and raising the thumb to mean no. Thus he combines the suggestive force of hypnosis with the seductions of babying, and in case the patient is reluctant to make up stories out loud, he smooths the way by allowing her just to raise a finger.

Not surprisingly, this procedure may produce an alter, but one is not enough. Putnam tells the patient to "expect that new alters will be found as therapy progresses." And he provides the opportunities for them to appear. If the patient experiences a sudden change of emotion, he asks, "Does this feeling have a name?"[7] He also gets her to do automatic writing and asks her to keep a journal, so that hidden alters will have a chance to sneak out. As each emerges, he asks him or her who else is in there.

Putnam, like many other MPD authorities, says that alters must not be treated as separate entities. Then, like other MPD authorities, he goes right ahead and treats them as separate entities—indeed, never lets them forget they are separate. The critical act is naming. As Janet pointed out over a century ago (and Putnam quotes him), naming solidifies an alter personality. Putnam insists that every alter be named, if not by the patient, then by the therapist. If the patient says it's "no one," then "No One" is that alter's name. (Compare Carlson's "Just Me.") Putnam also takes a history from each alter—age, sex, function, and so on—and he keeps a card file on them. Eventually he asks the patient to map what by now is her "personality system." "I have received Mercator projection maps, pie charts, architectural blueprints, organizational personnel charts," he says proudly.[8] He also conducts "inner group therapy," where all the alters assemble and battle it out. When decisions have to be made, he lets them vote—one alter, one vote. He sets up a "bulletin board" in the form of a notebook where they can leave messages for one another, thus reminding them that they are amnesic for one another. He videotapes them as they switch, thus facilitating switching. (Sometimes he works the camera. Sometimes he brings in a cameraman!) Then he shows them the videos. Not surprisingly, his patients soon become adept at switching.

Meanwhile, the patient is being rewarded at every turn for her new multiplicity and also for doing her other job as an MP, producing abuse memories. A potent reward is simply attention. Victim of an ancient crime, harborer of whole dynasties of warring identities, the patient becomes a sort of walking Greek tragedy, in which, before the therapist's riveted gaze, she plays all the parts. A wreck before, she is now a star, and like a star, she is filmed. Indeed, when she's not acting in films, she's making them. Putnam says that the retrieval of abuse memories can be made easier by the use of "screen techniques." The patient is hypnotized, the appropriate alter is called up, and the alter is asked to visualize a huge screen, on which she then replays her abuse memory, using freeze-frame, close-up, long shots, panning, slow motion, fast forward, zoom lens, even split screen. "This repertoire of camera techniques greatly facilitates the recovery of memories by allowing the patient to 'see' more than would be possible from a single point of view"[9]—in other words, by allowing her to fabricate. (Mind you, the story—for example, that she was raped by her uncle—will then be accepted by her and the therapist, and quite possibly presented to the uncle and his family as well, as factual truth, though Putnam, no doubt worried about this, discouraged patients from confronting their alleged abusers.) Offscreen too, she and the therapist can be creative together. Putnam doesn't just do regular hypnosis; he does "multilevel" hypnosis, hypnotizing the host, eliciting the alter, then hypnotizing the alter. He and the patient explore the "system": its "layering" (alters buried under alters), its "tree structures" (alters branching out from alters).

How can Putnam not see what is happening? That he is involved in what social psychologists call a role-enactment, whereby, if you give a person cues for a certain behavior, instructions as to how to perform the behavior, and rewards for the behavior, you will then get that behavior?[10] He never sees. He acknowledges that once the MPD diagnosis is made, "all of a sudden 'new' personalities begin popping out all over the place." He notes that many patients read up on MPD. (According to another authority, the patient sometimes knows more about the disorder than the therapist.) He says that the patient's amnesia sometimes turns out to be surprisingly leaky—that there's more communication going on among the alters than he was led to believe. He repeatedly points out that MPs are attention-seeking and manipulative. He describes their "chameleon-like abilities to bring out the personality who is most congruent to a given situation."[11]

But never, never does it occur to him that these factors, taken together, might suggest that the therapy is creating the patient's MPD. He notes that patients sometimes get their abuse histories mixed up—that they change the story, seemingly forgetting what they said before. The solution to this, he suggests, is to help them bring the stories into conformity, iron out the inconsistencies. All scientists are subject to "confirmation bias," to seeing what confirms their hypothesis and not seeing what would cast doubt on it, but never have I encountered a clearer example than Putnam's book. Nor do I believe there has ever been, on earth, a man more willing to credit the testimony of unsuccessful, out-of-control, desperate women, a large and unpopular group. Unfortunately, his faith is in the service of convincing them that they have multiple personality disorder.

Not only does Putnam have no doubts; like recovered-memory therapists, he quells any doubts on the part of the patient. "Not uncommonly," he reports, "patients will retreat into a phase during which they announce that they 'made it all up.'" This, he says, is called the "flight into health," and he interprets it to the patient as resistance to treatment. Another form of resistance is an inability to be hypnotized; this is "stonewalling," and it is a "poor prognostic sign," as is reluctance to accept the MPD diagnosis.[12] If the patient wants to get better, she must acknowledge that she is an MP, allow herself to be hypnotized, and lay her questions aside. It is an airtight system.

But Putnam, as I said, is a cautious man. Others are far bolder. Colin Ross doesn't just ask alters to come out; he begs them. He suggests the following appeal:

> I understand that you don't want to talk to me right now. That's fine. I'm certainly not going to try to force you. . . . Let me explain why I would like to talk to you. I just want to get to know you a bit. . . . One reason I would like to talk to you is to get your opinion on things.

Maybe there's something I'm doing that you don't like, that I could change if you told me about it. What I was thinking was, maybe if you don't feel like talking with me, you could write me a note.[13]

Ross also shows his patients educational videos about MPD, thus teaching them how to switch. Ralph Allison, one of the pioneers of the MPD movement, writes of hypnotizing a patient and ordering a suspected alter, "Come out by the time I count to three. One . . . Two . . . Three!"[14] (The alter came out.)

If Putnam generally limits himself to three-hour diagnostic interviews, that is brief. Richard Kluft cites a case in which "spontaneous" switching did not occur until the *eighth* continuous hour of questioning. Kluft adds that "interviewees must be prevented from taking breaks to regain composure, averting their eyes to avoid self-revelation, etc." (The South African psychiatrist Michael Simpson says that the examination methods recommended by MPD therapists closely resemble interrogation techniques that he has been asked to review in the context of human rights abuses.) If the therapist is not satisfied with the constellation of alters he has obtained, he can add to it—an achievement that was apparently first reported by the MPD pioneer Eugene Bliss: "I induced another personality, 'Dr. Bliss,' through hypnosis to assist me in therapy. This was done rapidly through hypnotic trance and my colleague, 'Dr. Bliss,' has been living with 30 other personalities since that date."[15] The number of alters can be further raised by sending the patient to an MPD group. (Remember Elizabeth Carlson's group, where everyone eventually developed a "Nikki.")

Once the alters are out, they are heavily rewarded. Ross cossets child alters, takes them to McDonald's. If a child alter brings a toy bear to a session, he says, the therapist should talk to the bear: "The therapist may comment on how brave the bear is, how lucky the bear is to have the child with him, and how glad the therapist is that the bear was willing to share these memories." As with

Putnam, the alters are constantly reminded that they are separate. Ross holds "inner board meetings" and takes roll. Kluft says that his most common hypnotic instruction is, "Everybody listen."[16]

Again and again in the literature the patient's sense of guilt is pressed into service to create new alters. Bennett Braun tells of saying to a patient who had had a rough night, "Will whoever picked up the man and let Mary find herself in bed with him, please be here and talk with me?" Kluft describes an episode in which a hospitalized patient, threatened with termination of treatment, told him that she had been getting telephone calls from "the cult" instructing her to kill him. He knew that she had been barred from use of the phone during the period in question, and he confronted her with the lie. As a result, he says, "I was able to access an alter who claimed to have given most of the personalities the hallucinated experience of such calls by means of autohypnosis."[17] He offers this story as an example of how, while others are gullible, he is not.

Hospital staffs are not always so willing to believe. Multiples are distinct non-favorites with nurses and orderlies. Putnam describes a hospitalized patient who one minute would go into a catatonic state, defecating in her hospital gown, and then next minute would be on the ward telephone ordering expensive clothes from local stores. The hospital staff, who had to clean her up, were impatient with this behavior, Putnam recalls sadly. They couldn't see it "as being due to different alters"; they regarded it as "deliberate manipulation."[18] This, he says, shows how skepticism about MPD makes it hard to hospitalize patients.

The threat of termination of treatment seems to be a powerful stimulus to the production of alters. The woman, cited earlier, who had 335 personalities, some of whom flew over the hospital, was Colin Ross's patient Pam. These hordes did not come forth, however, until Ross, having failed to get Pam to show full-fledged multiplicity, was considering transferring her to a state hospital. Then, suddenly, "Midge" appeared, followed by 334 others. Eventually, though, Pam's tie with Ross was broken; she was discharged to out-patient treatment with another therapist. Now disaster struck. Pam reported that her mother had committed suicide. Treatment went back into full gear. Pam and her therapist did two months of "grief work." Then, apparently, Pam tired of grief work, for "Bob," a new alter, emerged and told the therapist that Pam's mother was alive but that for various reasons he had convinced Pam otherwise. This was a bad idea, the therapist and Ross (he was consulting) told Bob. "Bob agreed that we should explain the whole thing to Pam; we asked him to go back inside, called Pam out, and delicately explained everything to her." Strange to say, Pam "shrugged the whole thing off." Still, the therapists did not doubt Bob's story. "Clearly, for Pam the suicide was a reality," Ross writes.[19]

That reality having vanished, Pam may have felt she needed fur-ther grounds for therapy. In any case, a new disaster struck: Pam reported that she had inoperable lung cancer. "She wore a scarf over her head, having experienced substantial hair loss [from chemother-apy], including loss of her eyebrows." This time, the therapists checked the story, and they found that Pam was not registered at the oncology clinic where she said she was being treated. Ross says that he and his colleague were amazed: "Someone inside was mak-ing Pam believe that she had cancer, and was shaving her eyebrows! We wanted to continue working with Pam, but an angry alter per-sonality began making death threats against the therapist, and we decided to stop therapy. She has been lost to further follow-up."[20] Nowhere in his narration of this failed therapy does Ross consider that the MPD diagnosis might have been wrong. Before she fell into his hands, Pam had been treated for borderline personality disorder. She had also received a diagnosis of manic-depressive illness. But Ross explained to her that the manic-depressive illness didn't really exist. It was part of her MPD; it was being manufactured by an alter.

How are we to understand a story such as this? Is the therapist humoring the patient, helping her spin a tale that he thinks will be therapeutic, even at the cost of its including, in the usual case, episodes of childhood sexual abuse and thus, in all probability, alienating her from her family? Sometimes it seems that this must be what is happening: the therapist sees the alters as metaphors. But as the reader discovers, that is not how the therapist sees it, or says it. According to most of the MPD literature, the alters are true dissociative phenomena, spontaneous and fascinating apparitions.

Ross, in his MPD casebook, tells us with great deliberation how child alters speak. It's "hard to describe," he says, but there is "a slight modification of 'r' sounds into 'w,' almost with a slight lisp." Others may find this easier to describe than Ross does. It is the way an adult speaks when pretending to be a child. ("I'm sowwy I bwoke the twuck.") Similarly crude theatricals can be sampled on any MPD documentary, in any MPD autobiography. In Jane Phillips's MPD memoir *The Magic Daughter*, the teenage alter "JJ" says things like "That's cool," while the child alters refuse to take their "med'cine." The therapist responds to them in an age-appropriate manner. (He reads the child alters stories.) Today, in the wake of the MPD scandals, Colin Ross is claiming that some people diagnosed as multiples were just "con artists."[21] If these primitive enactments were the con, then it took a special mentality to be fooled by them.

5

The Science

If the MPD case histories are shocking, the field's experimental literature is more so. Case histories are assumed to be biased, because the person reporting the case, the therapist, has a stake in it. Experimental research, on the other hand, is supposed to be set up in such a way as to eliminate bias, through such mechanisms as choosing subjects at random, comparing them to control groups (groups who have not undergone the experimental conditions), having results assessed "blind" (by people who don't know which group was which), and above all, by focusing on empirical findings, things that can be observed, verified.

Again and again, the MPD research dispenses with these safeguards. A nice example is a pair of surveys—one by Frank Putnam and his colleagues, one by Colin Ross and his colleagues, both from the late 1980s[1]—that supposedly established the connection between MPD and childhood abuse. In both studies, the researchers surveyed a large number of therapists, asking them, among other things, whether their MPD patients had reported childhood sexual abuse. In the Putnam group 83 percent of the patients reported sexual abuse; in the Ross group, 79 percent. But as it turns out, none of this abuse was verified. It was simply what the therapists chose to report about what their patients, on the basis of their fallible memories of childhood, had chosen to report, after treatment (three

years, on average, in the Putnam study[2]) with those very same therapists, all of whom were MPD enthusiasts—the American therapists in the Ross survey were all members of the ISSMP&D—and
most of whom, therefore, would have endorsed the abuse theory of
MPD and used the powerfully suggestive techniques we have
already discussed to extract their patients' "hidden" abuse memories. (The majority of the patients had been hypnotized prior to
diagnosis.) That is the status of the sexual abuse statistics that have
been repeated like a mantra from article to article to eliminate any
doubt as to the truth of the post-Sybil theory of MPD. In the words
of Ian Hacking, "Psychiatry did not discover that . . . child abuse
causes multiple personality. It forged that connection."[3]

To my knowledge, only one MPD researcher, Philip Coons of
the Indiana University School of Medicine, has tried consistently
over the years to obtain solid corroboration for abuse reports in
MPD patients. In a 1986 study of twenty patients, he got corroboration for seventeen; in a 1994 study of nine patients he got corroboration for three.[4] But in both cases, what was corroborated was
"abuse," physical and/or sexual. Children are physically abused every
day, and by today's definitions I and most of my childhood friends
would probably be considered to have a physical abuse history.
(That is, we were spanked often. That was discipline in the fifties.)
But the focus of MPD theory and therapy is *sexual* abuse. In the
words of Richard Kluft, "MPD is primarily a disorder of sexually
abused women."[5] In an interesting act of prestidigitation, some
MPD writers begin by giving a credibly high figure for "abuse"—
credible because it includes physical abuse—and then, soon after-
ward, are using this figure as if it applied to sexual abuse alone. One
of the least discussed subjects in the MPD literature is child beating. These people want to talk about sex.

Now, it must be said that sexual abuse is hard to corroborate.
Child-molesters, when asked, do not generally volunteer the truth,
and families tend to close ranks. One way for a researcher to get
around this problem is to work not from the present to the past but

in the opposite direction, beginning with records of documented abuse. This was the approach taken by Linda Meyer Williams, of the University of New Hampshire. Williams's concern was not with MPD specifically but with the general claim—on which MPD theory depends—that memory of childhood sexual trauma can be lost and then regained. Using the files of a Northeastern city hospital, she tracked down 129 adult women who had been treated there for verified sexual abuse between the ages of ten months and twelve years. She then put the women through a three-hour interview, purportedly a "follow-up study" of patients treated at that hospital, and in the process asked them about their history of childhood abuse. The people who did not recount the incident on file at the hospital.

Like the Putnam and Ross surveys with abuse causation, this study is routinely cited as evidence that abuse can be forgotten. What is rarely mentioned, outside critiques of RM and MPD, is that most of Williams's "forgetters" reported *other* incidents of sexual abuse. In all, 88 percent of the women interviewed said that they had been molested—a figure that suggests the very opposite of RM/MPD theory: childhood sexual abuse is very likely to be remembered. As for the remaining 12 percent, some, when abused, were probably too young to remember, and others may have been reluctant to recount their entire childhood sexual history to a stranger with a clipboard. (In a similar study, the researchers paid a return visit to all the "forgetters" whom they could find and asked them again about their abuse history, whereupon all of them supplied the missing information, saying that they hadn't wanted to talk about it before. As one woman put it, "I didn't want to say it cuz I wanted to forget. . . . I only cry when I think about it." This latter study, however, was of *physical* abuse. How much more likely that people would avoid discussing their histories of sexual abuse?) Yet ISSD (ISSMP&D) president Marlene Hunter, in a 1998 message to the membership of the organization, summarized the Williams study by saying that "a huge majority of the women remembered neither the [hospital] admission nor the abuse." Apart from the fact that 38 percent is not a majority, let alone a huge one, there is no evidence that the women did not remember—only that, possibly for excellent reasons, they did not report.[6]

The question of whether childhood abuse can be forgotten and then retrieved is the most aggrieved issue in RM/MPD, for on it depends the question of whether therapists are justified in digging for abuse memories in patients who report none. No one doubts that one episode of sexual abuse can drop out of memory and then resurface. Several of the pedophile-clergy scandals of the 1980s—cases in which the abuser did confess—were set off by adults who claimed they had forgotten and then remembered. But in those instances, the vast majority of the victims who eventually came forward said they had never forgotten.

Furthermore, what is at issue in the RM/MPD debates is not the forgetting of one episode, but the continuous repression, over years and years, of repeated abuse. In MPD cases, says Colin Ross, "The sexual abuse usually starts before age five, lasts more than ten years, involves more than one perpetrator, and includes at least vaginal intercourse and fellatio."[7] That is roughly what former Miss America (and current child-protection activist) Marilyn Van Derbur Atler reports: that from age five to eighteen she was regularly molested by her father and forgot each incident, one by one, for thirteen years. By night she was raped; by day, she was oblivious. This phenomenon, which Richard Ofshe calls "robust repression," has no scientific support whatsoever. No one has demonstrated that such a thing can occur. Nor, prior to the RM/MPD movement, had anyone dreamed that such a thing could occur, as Ofshe and Ethan Watters point out in their book *Making Monsters*. Why, Ofshe and Watters ask, are we "the first generation to document the fact that victims can walk away from endless brutalizing experiences with no knowledge that something bad has happened to them?" And as the Harvard memory researcher Daniel Schacter has pointed out in his comprehensive book *Searching for Memory*, hundreds of studies have demonstrated the exact opposite: "that repetition of information leads to improved memory, not loss of memory, for that information"[8]—a principle to which Auschwitz survivors, for example, can testify. They wish they could forget.

This wave of nonsupport for robust repression has occurred during a period of excited research on memory, prompted in part by the RM/MPD movement. The studies have led to four main conclusions, all of which should be depressing to people who think they know where they were when John F. Kennedy was killed, or indeed in the rest of their lives. First, memory deteriorates and often disappears inexorably. Second, memory changes over time, becoming a compound of real and imagined events. Third, memory can be altered, or actually created wholesale, by suggestion. Fourth, even experts cannot tell false memories from true without external verification. These findings have led to a thorough revision of psychologists' view of memory. Where they once believed in the "video-recorder" model, in which events were accurately recorded and accurately retrieved, now they have shifted to a "reconstructionist" model: memory is not remembered, it is created.

I will describe only one study.[9] When the space shuttle *Challenger* blew up in midair in 1986, Ulrich Neisser, a psychology professor at Emory University, realized that this terrible event would make for a good study of the stability of memory. The day after the explosion he asked the students in his introductory psychology class to write down what they were doing when they got the news. He collected the responses and put them in a drawer until 1988, two and a half years later, at which point he recontacted those students and asked them once again to write down what they were doing when they heard about the *Challenger* explosion. He then rated the 1988 responses for accuracy (that is, conformity to the 1986 responses) on a scale of 0 to 7. The average rating was 3, and one-fourth of the students got a zero. One woman who had reported in

1986 that she was told in the school cafeteria now said, "I was in my dorm room when some girl came running down the hall screaming." A man who had earlier said that he got the news at school now reported that he had been at home with his family. Even more interesting was the fact that when the poor-rememberers were shown their earlier accounts, they did not back down. One student, when shown his 1986 account, said, "This is my handwriting, so it must be right, but I still remember everything happening the way I told you [in 1988]. I can't help it."

If this is the status of memories that are only two and a half years old and have not been the focus of suggestive therapeutic procedures, what can we say of the accuracy of memories that are typically said to be at least twenty years old, that have been elicited and shaped by a trusted authority figure, that have been "abreacted" in highly emotional performances, and that have served as the justification for years of costly psychotherapy? It is surprising that retractors retract. Were it not for the recent memory research, showing how forgetful and suggestible we all are, they probably wouldn't. The loss of face would be too great.

Another weak spot in the scientific underpinning of MPD is research on the prevalence of child abuse. In some populations, claims of child abuse rose by 900 percent from 1976 to 1986—that is, during the height of the child protection movement—and they have gone on rising. This increase is of course a reaction to under-estimates in earlier decades. It is also intended as a corrective to government statistics, which are unquestionably too low—the government's 1995 finding for child abuse in general is 1.6 percent—because they are based only on *reported* abuse. But as the figures rise, one must look at the definitions of abuse on which they are based. A 1985 survey of women in Los Angeles found that 62 percent had been sexually abused, with abuse broadly defined as anything from rape to unwanted sexual remarks before age eighteen. The following year, a review of prevalence studies cited another survey of Los Angeles women in which it was found that 6 percent had been sexually abused, with abuse narrowly defined as forced sexual contact before age sixteen.[10] Many RM/MPD writers just say one-third, an average of the high and low figures, and neglect to mention the liberality of the definition that led to the high figures. (They also focus, again and again, on father–daughter incest, despite the fact that this seems to be one of the rarest forms of childhood sexual abuse.) But in a time when, according to the newspapers, tens of thousands of children are being sold by their families to brothel-owners in Cambodia, Vietnam, Taiwan, China, India, and the Philippines, is it not frivolous to say that a well-fed American girl to whom someone has made a dirty remark is an abuse victim?

Another tormented question is whether childhood sexual abuse causes any kind of adult psychopathology—forget MPD. Here again, the believers tend to assemble their findings by working backward. They get a woman who has some problem that their literature says is often connected with childhood sexual abuse. (Bulimia is a favorite, but as we saw earlier, there is almost no psychological problem that RM/MPD people do not see as stemming from sexual abuse. Judith Herman claims that in dealing with patients who have histories of alcohol or drug dependency, not to ask about incest "amounts to negligence."[11]) Then, through hypnosis or whatever, they obtain an abuse story from her. The story is then taken as evidence that abuse causes adult psychopathology.

But there is little or no research support for this claim, as Frank Putnam himself has pointed out. (In his book *Dissociation in Children and Adolescents* he writes, "As yet, no psychiatric disorder has been proven to be 'caused' by childhood maltreatment.") Many studies have found that people reporting childhood sexual abuse show higher levels of psychological disturbance and general unhappiness than people not reporting sexual abuse. But when the subjects are matched with controls on "family dysfunctionality"—that is, when people who come from terrible families that abused them sexually are compared with people who come from families equally terrible except that they didn't abuse them sexually—the two groups' psychopathology rates turn out to be approximately equal. One 1994 study tried to separate the effects of five kinds of mal-treatment: physical abuse, physical neglect, verbal abuse, emotional neglect, and sexual abuse. The findings suggested that the most damaging is emotional neglect. As for sexual abuse, a recent report, summarizing many studies, says, "A substantial number of these investigations find that a majority of victims suffer no extensive harm."[12]

Many people view this finding with repugnance. So do I. (For one thing, even if only a minority suffer harm, that is still a prob-lem.) According to Ian Hacking, in *Rewriting the Soul*, our discom-fort is rooted in "consequentialist ethics,"[13] the idea that for something to be bad, it must have bad results. Adults who engage children in sex, Hacking says, should be condemned on absolute grounds, regardless of the consequences for the child. Most people would agree with him—I do—but such a position has no bearing on the claim that childhood sexual abuse causes multiple personal-ity disorder.

A final baseless claim of the MPD writers is that the disorder can be cured by the prescribed treatment, focusing on alters and abuse memories. "Strictly speaking, there are no treatment outcome data in the literature," Colin Ross writes in his MPD textbook. This does not prevent him from asserting, six pages later, that three-quarters of MPs can be "treated to integration in less than $2\frac{1}{2}$ years"[14]—an opinion seconded by many other MPD authorities. (Cornelia Wilbur, 1984: When treated by a "knowledgeable therapist," MPs have "an excellent prognosis." Margo Rivera, 1992: MPs "can be completely healed." Bennett Braun, 1986: "MPD has an excellent prognosis if intense psychotherapy is available."[15]) Not only are there no controlled studies to support these confident statements, there are copious indications to the contrary. In his own casebook, *The Osiris Complex*, Ross records only three cures among the eigh-teen MPs whose treatment he describes. And like Elizabeth Carl-son, many patients seem to get considerably worse. George

Ganaway says that he has evaluated a number of patients who have been through MPD therapy: "After the daily reliving of trauma memories, these people are basket cases."[16]

But if there are no studies showing that MPD can be cured, there are very few studies of MPD in general. "All we get on this disorder are war stories, anecdotes, composite cases," says memory researcher John Kihlstrom. "It is *appalling* how little research there's been."[17] The MPD experts seem unbothered by this—and unaware that they are the ones who should be doing the research. In his 1989 textbook Ross prophesied, "Over the next 10 years a substantial body of clinical research on dissociation will be generated." What does he do with this statement when, almost ten years later, in revising the book, he has to deal with the fact that the deadline has not been met? Like an end-of-the-worlder, he just pushes back the deadline: "Over the next 10 years the already substantial body of clinical research will be much expanded." In the meantime he challenges others to refute the MPD community's unsupported claims: "The burden of proof that MPD is artifactual . . . lies on the shoulders of the skeptics," he declares.[18] This is as if Darwin had stayed home from the Galapagos and told *others* to try to refute the theory of natural selection.

≫ ≪

Reading the MPD literature, one gets the impression that these writers don't actually care about science. At least since the sixties, when many people without advanced scientific training entered the field of psychotherapy, there has been a science-versus-practice war in psychology, with the researchers claiming that the therapists operate without any scientific grounding and the therapists claiming that the researchers have no idea what it means to treat a patient. In the eyes of many therapists, to ask that treatment be guided by scientific truths is to make a cold, left-brain argument— one that, the feminists would add, is highly characteristic of males. When Richard Ofshe and Ethan Watters, in an interview with

Ellen Bass, asked about scientific support for the teachings of *The Courage to Heal,* she replied, "Look, if we waited for scientific knowledge to catch up, we could just forget the whole thing. My ideas are not based on any scientific theories."[19]

But in the MPD field, this kind of thinking is embraced also by the experts, the textbook-writers, the MDs. Putnam, a medical doctor on staff at the National Institute of Mental Health, says in his textbook that while the link between abuse and MPD remains unproven, "no therapist who has worked with more than two or three multiples doubts the existence of a causal relationship between MPD and childhood trauma, primarily child abuse." So it's like jazz or orgasm—you just know it when you see it. On the subject of verification of abuse claims, Dan Sexton, director of the National Child Abuse Hotline, once said to an audience, "I'm not a law enforcement person, thank God! I'm a psychology person, so I don't need the evidence."[20] Many of his colleagues clearly agree with him.

But if the MPD experts wanted to do scientific research on this disorder, they would have a problem. A scientific theory has to be *falsifiable:* to be proven true, it must be capable of being proven false. MPD theory is not of this kind. The disorder is described in *DSM* in terms of overt symptoms, but as we saw, the patients very rarely present with such symptoms. That, says Richard Kluft, is because MPD is not really a set of behaviors but an "intrapsychic structure"—and one that hides itself from diagnosticians, in various ways. There is "secret" MPD, Kluft tells us, and "latent," "private," and "covert" MPD. (These are all different.) There is also "isomorphic MPD," in which the alter or alters appear "indistinguishable" from the host personality. In such a case, says Kluft, "it is very difficult to suspect the presence of MPD"—and no wonder. In addition, there is a large category of "phenocopy MPD," in which the patient appears to have a different disorder but really has MPD. Kluft is not the only believer in "phenocopy MPD." Colin Ross proposes that many people diagnosed with schizophrenia, depression, anorexia, obsessive-compulsive disorder, and neurological disorders—plus transvestites, transsexuals, and sex offenders—are probably multiples. He adds that if AIDS is spreading, that could be because many HIV-positive people have MPD, and the alter who learns about safe sex is different from the alter who has sex.[21]

All these special variants of MPD have one thing in common: they justify the diagnosis of MPD in patients who show no multiplicity. In the words of August Piper, "If the 'entity' [alter] shows itself, then the patient has MPD. But if it fails to show itself, then the patient still has MPD." A corollary is that MPD can be detected only by someone who truly believes in the disorder. In the face of a nonbeliever, the "sensitive alters," as Kluft calls them, will go on hiding, and the patient will languish without help. (Apropos of this, Michael Simpson quotes *Peter Pan:* "Every time a child says: 'I don't believe in fairies,' there is a fairy somewhere that falls down dead.") The other corollary is that the MPD-suspecting diagnostician must aggressively *seek* MPD. Hence the leading questions, the marathon interviews, the hypnosis.[22]

≫ ≪

The study of MPD, then, is not a science but a belief system. And like other belief systems, it has become more entrenched in the face of criticism. "The charge of artifact" against MPD, Ross says, is "a second line of defense against dealing with the reality of child abuse in North America." And why might people not want to deal with that reality? One possibility, insisted upon by some feminists, is that doubters are part of the backlash against the women's movement. In the words of Judith Herman, "Violence against women and children . . . is a privilege that men do not relinquish easily." Another possibility, Betsy Petersen has suggested in her incest memoir, is that they too have been abused—or have abused. But wittingly or unwittingly, they are protecting sex criminals. They are also retraumatizing survivors. In the third edition of *The Courage to Heal*, Bass and Davis introduce their new section on the "back-lash" (RM skepticism) by warning the reader that she may find this material "overwhelming" and should put the book down if she can't stand it.[23]

Skeptics, it is said, are making common cause with violent tyrannies. Bass and Davis compare childhood abuse to "the gassing of the Kurds, the massacre at My Lai, the rape of women in Bosnia." E. Sue Blume, in refusing to be silent on the subject of sexual abuse, compares herself to the solitary dissident who faced down the tanks in Tiananmen Square. But the most frequent comparison is of course to the Holocaust. Elizabeth Loftus, whose memory research has contributed to the critique of the RM movement, writes of hav-ing received a letter telling her to "please consider your work to be on the same level as those who deny the existence of the extermi-nation camps during World War II." Bass and Davis end their book by appropriating for recovered memory Elie Wiesel's words on the death camps: "To forget would mean to kill the victims a second time."[24]

In part, RM/MPD is a liberationist movement, akin to the "human potential" movement of the sixties. Bass and Davis, in *The Courage to Heal*, advise the reader to dance her feelings. They invite her to experience "the scary miracle of being able to stay present." They tell her that when she acknowledges her abuse, she will release untapped potential that will transform not only her own life but the world: "Imagine all the women healed—and all that energy no longer used for mere survival but made available for . . . freeing political prisoners, ending the arms race." Environmentalism too will be served. "How many pedophiles care about toxic waste?" Bass and Davis ask.[25]

But liberationism has its tougher side too. Judith Herman writes that many trauma therapists close ranks, go "underground" if nec-essary. "We believe our patients," she quotes one therapist saying. "We just don't tell our supervisors." To doubt a patient's abuse story,

Herman says, is "identification with the perpetrator." The therapist must "affirm a position of moral solidarity with the survivor."[26] Particularly in the eighties, the RM/MPD workers, like the Pentecostals with whom they joined hands, viewed themselves as a grassroots campaign, an uprising of decent, embattled people against a powerful "establishment" enemy. They saw hidden machinations. They decried cover-ups. Their enemy's enemy, no matter how questionable, was their friend. And it was this paranoid edge that made the movement vulnerable to the thing that would so damage it, the satanic ritual abuse craze.

6

The Crisis

Like the MPD movement, the satanic ritual abuse (SRA) epidemic of the 1980s was kicked off by a mass-market book, *Michelle Remembers*, by Michelle Smith and Lawrence Pazder. Smith was a Canadian housewife, Pazder a psychiatrist she had consulted for several years about depression. In 1976, at age twenty-seven, Smith returned to Dr. Pazder, sensing that she had some unfinished business, and in a year's worth of trance sessions she recovered her memory, repressed for more than two decades, of having been tortured at age five by a satanic cult of which her mother was a priestess. Briefly, the satanists starved her, vomited on her, sodomized her, electroshocked her, forced her to drink her own urine, drove her into a rock embankment in an exploding automobile, stuck snakes up her vagina, gave her rubdowns with bloody gobbets of cut-up dead people, and dumped her in an open grave and threw dead kittens on her. After a year of this, they let her go, and she went back to school and forgot the whole thing until her sessions with Dr. Pazder twenty-two years later. In 1980 Smith and Pazder published their account of this. Later they divorced their respective spouses and married each other.

In recent years, *Michelle Remembers* has been widely smirked at. Michelle's two sisters, unmentioned in the text—one older than she, one younger—have come forward to ask how they were kept in ignorance of the crimes visited on their sibling. Nevertheless, the book was influential. Soon after its publication the day-care scandals of the early 1980s erupted, with children claiming, often under aggressive questioning, that they had suffered tortures similar to Michelle's: their day-care handlers had molested them, urinated on them, made them participate in baby-murders and other satanic revels. But by this time adult women were also reporting such memories, often as part of RM therapy. And if the therapist believed in SRA and questioned the patient about it, the satanic memories were that much more likely to surface. As hypnosis expert Michael Yapko described it on the *Frontline* "Divided Memories" documentary, "What might have started out as a simple experience of sexual abuse, by weeks later it's satanic ritual abuse. 'Our dad killed the pizza delivery guy and made us eat his gall bladder.' And the stories just get more and more bizarre." We saw this in the case of Elizabeth Carlson.

The SRA craze has now been analyzed by a number of writers—Joel Best, David Bromley, Sherrill Mulhern, Debbie Nathan, James Richardson, Jeffrey Victor, Lawrence Wright, together with historians of RM and MPD. The causes appear to have been much the same as those of RM and MPD: family breakdown, the child protection movement, fundamentalism, pornography, the culture wars, feminism and reactions to feminism. In the case of SRA, however, fundamentalism was doubly important. Many SRA claimants came from strict Christian backgrounds, as did a number of the front-line warriors against the supposed satanic cults. That makes sense; these people believe in Satan. Also crucial was the religious right's campaign against feminism. As noted, it was day-care centers, the places where women who were going off to work left their children, that were fingered in many of the early reports as the satanists' headquarters. Some writers have also suggested that the dead-baby imagery so common in SRA stories arose from the abortion debate.

Jeffrey Victor sees SRA as "an attempt to restore an idealized society to past greatness and moral purity" by blaming a single, outside enemy for the decline of old-time values. The fall of the USSR no doubt had an effect as well. Absent that enemy, feelings of cultural embattlement had to find a new object, and SRA supplied it. With the satanic cults, Bennett Braun told an audience, "we are working with a national-international type organization that's got a structure somewhat similar to the communist cell structure, where it goes from . . . small groups to local councils, regional councils, district councils, national councils."[1]

Not just in its causes but in many other respects, SRA resembled MPD. It had the same odd distribution: the claimants were mostly women, overwhelmingly North American, and they tended to come out of the office of a small number of therapists. In one large survey, 5 percent of the clinicians reported 58 percent of the SRA cases. Like MPD, SRA spread to therapists via workshops and conferences, to patients via therapy and group therapy, and to both via the media. From 1988 to 1990, Geraldo Rivera produced a long series of enthusiastic shows on SRA. He opened one as follows: "Satanic cults: every hour, every day, their ranks are growing. . . . The odds are that this is happening in your town." The women in Elizabeth Carlson's MPD group would make videotapes of Geraldo's SRA shows and trade the tapes with each other.[2]

As with MPD, if you denied SRA, you were "in denial" and indifferent to the suffering of children, and possibly a perpetrator. D. Corydon Hammond told the Fourth Annual Eastern Regional Meeting on Abuse and Multiple Personality that "people who believe ritual abuse is not real are either naive . . . or they are dirty." But by the mid-eighties SRA was not only like MPD; it was part of the MPD movement. Braun, it will be remembered, was Patricia Burgus's therapist; D. Corydon Hammond was the man who debriefed Mary Shanley on her cult crimes. A 1986 survey of ISSMP&D conference participants found that one-fourth of their patients were reporting cult abuse.[3] That year, nine papers on SRA, all unskeptical, were presented at the conference. For therapists, the ISSMP&D eventually became the major source of SRA contagion.

There is an important difference, though, between MPD and SRA, and that is in plausibility. If many of the MPD stories are hard to believe, most of the SRA stories are frankly ludicrous. Like Sybil, Michelle was outdone by her successors. Judith Spencer's popular book *Suffer the Child* tells the purportedly true story of Jenny Walters Harris, whose cult experiences included being nailed to a cross. A clergyman who came to her house to perform an exorcism found "legions of demons . . . lining the driveway." (Harris eventually developed more than four hundred alters, including Blair, a three-foot-tall man with one eye; Mindoline, a devil with no skin; and Flisha, an attractive young woman who enjoyed "opera, symphony, museums, reading.") This is not to mention the usual claims: of robed cultists fornicating on altars, of priests collecting blood, semen, and urine in chalices for group libations, of people dining on babies. Using the figure of 10,000 murders per year—a low estimate, according to some SRA believers—sociologist David Bromley calculated that the period covered by the current survivors' claims would have produced 400,000 victims.[4] Strange to say, almost nobody went to the police.

Eventually, the police went to them. In the mid-eighties the FBI initiated a full-scale investigation of SRA, examining the evidence in over three hundred alleged crimes by organized cults. Investigators could not obtain corroboration for a single one. The National Center on Child Abuse and Neglect did a similar study, and again could produce no evidence. These findings were all the more remarkable in that murder, unlike child-molesting, tends to leave evidence. Furthermore, it leaves somebody *missing*. Finally, the supposed cult murderers were said to have had numerous accomplices. To accept the SRA accounts, one had to believe that among the thousands of participants in these murders, not a single person repented, slipped up, broke ranks, and took the police to the place where the bones were buried. "If this is true," said Kenneth

Lanning, head of the FBI investigation, "it's the greatest conspiracy in the history of mankind."[5]

For MPD believers, SRA created a crisis similar to the one faced by American Communists when news of the Moscow trials reached the West in the late thirties. They had two choices. They could defend SRA, which by the end of the 1980s put them in the position of kooks, like UFO believers. Or they could repudiate SRA, which meant abandoning their colleagues and saying that their enemies had been right. Worse, it meant casting doubt not just on SRA but on MPD and recovered memory, for the therapeutic procedures that had produced the SRA stories—indeed, in many cases, the patients who had produced the SRA stories   were the same ones that had produced MPD. If the therapists did not believe an alter who said her father raped her and then made her eat a baby, why did they believe an alter who, under the same conditions (hypnosis, coercive questioning) just said her father raped her? To reject SRA was to admit the strong possibility that MPD was produced not by abuse and dissociation but, like SRA, by the media, by the rumor mill, and above all by therapy.

Actually, many MPD believers of the 1980s had never been SRA believers, but they too understood what SRA meant with regard to MPD, and they began walking away from MPD. George Ganaway took the prevailing MPD theory seriously for a while in the mid-eighties, but in 1989, in the face of the SRA scandal, he published a paper claiming that many SRA stories were probably "screen memories" masking recollections of far more ordinary cruelty, real or imagined.[6] He also expressed reservations about MPD. Today, in treating dissociative patients, he does not address "alters"; he practices traditional psychodynamic therapy. A more striking defection was that of Frank Putnam, author of the "classic text" on MPD. As Putnam explained to me, that book's publication was delayed. Though it came out in 1989, it was written in 1986, after which Putnam changed the focus of his research from MPD to dissociation in general—that is, something that demonstrably exists—

and from adults to children and adolescents—that is, patients whose trauma history can often be verified. The reason for the switch, he told me, was the difficulty in tracking the trauma in MPD patients. In the book, however, he had no problem with his MPD patients' trauma memories. Remember his words: "No therapist who has worked with more than two or three multiples doubts the existence of a causal relationship between MPD and childhood trauma, primarily child abuse." It seems to have been the *new* kind of trauma memories, satanic ritual abuse memories, that broke his confidence.

So, as with the Moscow trials, the moderates walked out and the hard-liners stayed—and took a harder line. Extremism swamped the field. The leader was Bennett Braun. (Ganaway calls Braun and his colleague Roberta Sachs the "Typhoid Marys" of the satanic abuse craze.[7]) The satanic cult that Braun descried involved the Ku Klux Klan, the neo-Nazis, organized crime, big business, the CIA, and the military, together with AT&T and the FTD Florists. His MPD patients, Braun said, had had their alters programmed into them by the cult when they were children. Now they had wandered into his care, and the cult was trying to reclaim them. One way was by sending coded floral bouquets to hospitalized patients. But Braun had cracked the code, and, to the audience at the 1992 Midwestern Conference on Child Sexual Abuse and Incest, he revealed it: "Pink flowers mean suicide, red means cutting. Red roses or white baby's breath mean bloody suicide. Pink roses mean hanging. Blue is death by suffocation. . . . If the card is signed 'Love you,' then that is a danger signal."[8]

The SRA cultists, needless to say, were not happy about Braun's telling their secrets. "About twenty patients have told me they were sent to kill me," he said to a journalist. He was taking precautions: he had placed his house in trust and changed his utilities accounts to someone else's name. He pointed out that he considered carefully before accepting a patient's SRA story. He applied what he called his "rule of five." If details in the story matched details in five other, independent SRA stories, then it was true. (He seems to have believed that fewer than five people in the United States watched *Geraldo*.) As for who the cultists were, here Braun had developed his "twelve Ps." Those perpetrating satanic ritual abuse were: "Pimps, Pushers, Prostitutes, Physicians, Psychiatrists, Psychotherapists, Principals and teachers, Pallbearers [meaning undertakers], Public workers, Police, Politicians and judges, and Priests and clergies from all religions."[9]

Colin Ross offered a different theory. In a 1993 proposal for a book to be called *CIA Mind Control*, he claimed that it was not a satanic conspiracy but rather the CIA that was turning children into "Manchurian candidates" via "drugs including hallucinogens, sensory deprivation, flotation tanks, electric shock. The programming involved the deliberate creation of multiple personality disorder with specific letter, number, and other access codes for contacting alter personalities." (Actually, during the Cold War period, the CIA did try, and fail, to create "killing machines" by means of drugs. Pendergrast believes that Ross got his theory out of *The Search for the "Manchurian Candidate,"* John Marks's 1979 book on this fiasco.) Ross has suggested that the current wave of skepticism about MPD was engineered by CIA operatives—that they know he has uncovered their plot and are therefore trying to discredit him and his specialty.[10] Hacking, in *Rewriting the Soul*, says that at meetings of families accused of child abuse people have been told that, in case of a lawsuit, they will be lucky if Ross testifies for the other side. In Vynette Hamanne's suit against Diane Humenansky, Ross did testify for the other side (for Humenansky), and according to some observers, his explanation of his "Manchurian candidate" theory was a major factor in the court's awarding Hamanne $2.7 million.

I have already mentioned D. Corydon Hammond's theory: that a Jewish doctor who collaborated with the Nazis and escaped to the United States now heads a vast conspiracy in which children are programmed via Greek letters. Like Braun with his floral iconography, Hammond laid bare the code. "Alpha represents general programming," as he described it to the Fourth Annual Regional

Conference on Abuse and Multiple Personality Disorder in 1992. "Beta appears to be sexual programs such as how to perform oral sex in a certain way. . . . Delta are killers. . . . Theta are psychic killers," and so on. Lest they forget which victims have been robotized how, the cultists carry laptop computers with records of all past programming. Hammond's cult involves the CIA, the Mafia, Hollywood, big business, and government leaders, together with many ordinary citizens whose job it is to cover up evidence of cult tortures. "Morticians are involved in many cases," says Hammond, and "physicians who can sign phony death certificates." (Other SRA believers assert that the cults carry around portable crematoria to destroy the evidence, and employ plastic surgeons to remove telltale scars. The police, it is said, are also in on the cult. Lanning, head of the FBI investigation, has been accused of satanism.) Like Braun, Hammond is concerned about the cult's reaction to his revelations, but he is undaunted. He opened his 1992 lecture by saying, "I've finally decided—to hell with it, if the cults are going to kill me, then they are going to kill me," an announcement that drew loud applause from the audience.[11] Reading about these new MPD theories—grand-scale, multinational, with laptop-toting satanists and Hollywood tie-ins—one is almost nostalgic for the old-style abuse stories, with Uncle Joe out by the woodshed. At least they were about human things: sex, weakness, sorrow.

⫸ ⫷

How many people in the MPD field believed these new theories? It is hard to tell, but according to Lawrence Wright, a 1991 survey of members of the American Psychological Association found that 30 percent had treated at least one SRA patient; on a second survey 93 percent of the SRA treaters said they believed these patients' claims to be true.[12] Those surveys were of psychologists in general; belief in SRA among MPD specialists was unquestionably higher.

Again, feminists were among the believers. In 1993 Ms. published a story in which a woman described her torture by a cult and asserted that SRA was another arm of the patriarchy.[13] (This despite the fact that in her story—and in very many SRA accounts, notably *Michelle Remembers*—the major abusers are women.) "If we want to stop ritual abuse," says the display copy accompanying the piece, "the first step is to believe these brutal crimes occur." Feminists in the RM movement quickly fell into step. In the third edition of *The Courage to Heal* Bass and Davis added a section called "Facing Sadistic Ritual Abuse." In the resource guide at the end of the book, they recommend *Michelle Remembers* and also *Suffer the Child*, with the devils in the driveway. How strange it is to see educated women place their faith in these lurid tales. Strange, too, to see Jews (Bass and Davis, for example) credit stories so similar to the ancient "blood libel" of anti-Semitism, whereby Jews were in league with the devil, used the blood of Christian children to make matzo, and therefore deserved to be killed. But what is most amazing is to see feminists support a movement so conservative, so alarmed about sex, so concerned with the supposed endangerment of females, who clearly, for their own protection, should not go out in the world and, above all, should not place their children in day care.

How could the feminists have missed the point? Well, the eighties was a period of vigorous backlash against feminism. In that tormented context, many feminists clearly felt that any woman alleging abuse, even by a devil with a tail, had to be believed. But the main reason was probably the difficulty stated before: to doubt SRA was to doubt recovered memory. Recovered memory was very important to feminism.

The Outcry

The craze over satanic ritual abuse irreparably weakened the MPD movement, made it look foolish. By the early nineties multiple personality disorder and recovered memory were facing attacks from all sides. The most important development was the founding of the False Memory Syndrome Foundation (FMSF) in Philadelphia in 1992. As Nicholas Spanos pointed out in his book on MPD, the witchcraft panics of the sixteenth and seventeenth centuries tended to fizzle out, in any given community, once the accusations "spiraled up the social scale and involved the families of people who wielded social power."[1] That is what happened with recovered memory. Spurred by early legal victories, accusations of abuse multiplied in the early 1990s. Among the accused was a mathematics professor at the University of Pennsylvania, Peter Freyd. In 1990 Freyd's daughter, Jennifer Freyd, a psychology professor at the University of Oregon—and subsequently the author of a book on recovered memory, *Betrayal Trauma*—claimed that with the help of her therapist she had remembered that her father had sexually abused her throughout her childhood, from fondling at age three to rape at age sixteen. (She has never retracted the substance of these accusations.) Peter Freyd denied the charges, and Pamela Freyd—Peter's wife, Jennifer's mother, and another Ph.D.—decided to establish an organization to help families faced with such accusations.

The FMSF's target was what it called "false memory syndrome," defined as "a condition in which a person's identity and interpersonal relationships are centered around a memory of traumatic experience which is objectively false but in which the person strongly believes." Pamela Freyd assembled an advisory board including some of the most respected psychologists and psychiatrists in the country. With the help of publicity in the local press, the FMSF in its first year was contacted by almost five thousand families accused of abuse on the basis of recovered memory. (By 1999 it had received calls from about twenty thousand families.) The organization sponsors conferences, sends out a monthly newsletter, and advises families. Pamela Freyd does not claim that every family calling the FMSF is innocent. "We don't know the truth or the falsity of any of the reports we receive," she says. "The problem is with the ways the abuse memories were obtained—hypnosis, sodium amytal, dream interpretation, guided imagery. It has been shown again and again that such techniques can produce false memories."[2]

The FMSF unified and galvanized what, up till then, had been the far-flung voices opposing RM, MPD, and SRA. Also, under the rubric of "false memory syndrome," it converted what for most accused families had been a private disaster—something that, however blameless, they would conceal at all costs—into a public matter, a social contagion, something that they could admit had struck their house. And so they began to fight back: talk to journalists, send private investigators with body tapes to their daughters' therapists, even write books. Pendergrast, author of *Victims of Memory*, is among the accused, and he has made no secret of this.

At the same time, the beginning of the nineties, criticism of MPD within the profession was mounting at a furious pace. Herbert Spiegel came forward with the Sybil story. In the *Harvard Mental Health Letter* Paul McHugh, director of psychiatry at Johns Hopkins, called for an immediate end to MPD treatment: "Close the dissociation services and disperse the patients to general psychiatric units. Ignore the alters. Stop talking to them, taking notes on them, and discussing them in staff conferences. Pay attention to real present problems and conflicts rather than fantasy." In the *British Journal of Psychiatry* the Canadian psychiatrist Harold Merskey reviewed the most celebrated MPD cases of the nineteenth and twentieth centuries and argued that not one of them (including Eve, whom many skeptics tend to accept) showed multiplicity without coaching from the therapist. "It is likely that MPD never occurs as a spontaneous persistent natural event in adults," he concluded.[3]

In some writings a note of real derision set in. In his book on MPD the psychologist Ray Aldridge-Morris quotes one reply to his survey of his British colleagues as to whether they had encountered the disorder: "In the UK, we react to any suggestion by patients or relatives that there are two or more personalities by immediately saying that there are two or more aspects to one personality, and asserting that the individual must take responsibility for both of these aspects. It works." (The British tend to suspect multiples of faking, whereas American skeptics generally ascribe the disorder to unconscious role-playing.) Many observers began to worry about what MPD was going to do to the reputation of psychotherapy. "Some malignant being simultaneously interested in striking a killing blow to psychiatry and to the law would regard MPD as a godsend," wrote the Seattle psychiatrist August Piper.[4]

As criticism mounted within the profession, the press reversed itself—on a dime, in some instances. In 1991, *Time* published a trusting and righteous article on the new incest-rememberers. In 1993, just two years later, the magazine printed a skeptical cover story on recovered memory, called "Lies of the Mind," warning that the RM movement might do "irreparable damage" to the psychotherapy profession. Other magazines now picked up the scandal for the first time. In 1992 *Playboy* carried Debbie Nathan's alternately hilarious and horrifying account of her experiences at a marathon retreat for abuse-survivors. ("Cathy said she'd been in a cult where she killed three children. Babies! And not only did she wield the fatal knife but she also excised the livers. Of her own kids!") In 1993, the *New Yorker* published Lawrence Wright's two-part article on Paul Ingram, including the account of Richard Ofshe's prompting Ingram to "remember" that he had forced his son and daughter to have sex with each other—the first clear demonstration that abuse memories, indeed abuse confessions, could be created by suggestion. In 1994 the *New York Review of Books* published a full-scale, frontal attack on recovered memory—again in two parts—by Frederick Crews, the well-known critic of Freud.[5]

Local stories of RM and MPD scandals went out over the wire services. The lawsuit brought by Nadean Cool (the woman with the duck alter) of Appleton, Wisconsin, against her therapist Kenneth Olson was reported on in faraway New York, by the *Daily News*, under the headline, "Devil Doc a Crock?" Several newspapers enthusiastically described the exorcism that Olson performed on Cool, a ceremony to which he brought a fire extinguisher because, he said, "sometimes Satan leaves rings of fire." The $10.6 million settlement of Patricia Burgus's lawsuit against Bennett Braun and the others was reported on the front page of the *New York Times*. At the same time there was a flood of denunciatory books on MPD, RM, and SRA. Some latecomer abuse memoirs were still published, but they tended to be harshly reviewed. *The Kiss*, Kathryn Harrison's 1997 account of her affair with her father, was described by James Wolcott in the *New Republic* as "kitsch," "trash." Even the temperate *New York Times* wondered how, if Harrison's experience was so damaging, she had managed to go on to such a successful writing career.[6]

But as in the rise of MPD, so in its fall, television was undoubtedly more important than print journalism. Together with, or in place of, survivors, retractors were now featured on the talk shows. In late 1995, Geraldo Rivera apologized on his program for his contributions to the RM and SRA epidemics.[7] Public television produced long, hair-raising programs on MPD, RM, and SRA. On *Frontline*'s "Search for Satan," Patricia Burgus told how Bennett

Braun rehearsed her to do her "switching" for the local news. "I was supposed to talk about how if it wasn't for Dr. Braun I wouldn't be alive," she added. CBC's "Mistaken Identities" included interviews with the victims of the Parry Sound MPD outbreak that followed Dale Ault's attendance at Margo Rivera's workshops. One patient reports that when she finally told Ault that she had never been abused, that the memories were false, he replied, "Which personality am I talking to now?" As a result of therapy, this patient says, "I almost lost my children, my family's destroyed, I'm an alcoholic, I'm a drug addict." Even Hollywood began backpedaling. In the most recent MPD movie, the 1996 *Primal Fear*, a murderer, having escaped conviction on the grounds that he had MPD, turns out to have faked the disorder.

But the most dramatic reversal occurred in the courts, as the wave of RM lawsuits (patients suing alleged abusers) gave way to an opposing wave of negligence and malpractice suits (patients suing therapists). In addition to those already described—Elizabeth Carlson, Patricia Burgus, Mary Shanley—there was the case of Renee Althaus in Pittsburgh, where the therapist, Judith Cohen, though doubting Althaus's cult memories, did not speak up even as Althaus's father was taken off to jail. The case was settled in 1994 for $272,000 in damages. In Oregon there was Patricia Rice who, having gone to a hypnotherapist, Gina Gamage, in order to lose weight and stop smoking, came out with memories of satanic abuse. In 1992 Rice, believing that a "good witch" was "telepathically directing her to safety," drove her car into oncoming traffic, killing a man. Tried for manslaughter, she was found "guilty but insane." She then sued Gamage, who settled for $425,000 plus $1,570 a month for the rest of Rice's life.

As these cases multiplied, with attendant publicity, the RM suits receded. By 1996 they had dropped back down almost to their 1989 level. Those that were filed were often dismissed or withdrawn. In the False Memory Syndrome Foundation's newsletter for January

1997, there were three pages of fine print listing the legal victories for the preceding year: RM suits thrown out, malpractice suits settled, licenses suspended. In view of rulings in many courts that "recovered memories" lacked the scientific support to meet legal standards of evidence—and also the Supreme Court's 1995 ruling that ideas introduced by expert scientific witnesses had to be "derived by the scientific method" and "supported by the appropriate validation" (which recovered memory is not)—the trend seemed likely to continue. Week by week, recovered memory and multiple personality disorder were discredited.[8]

The Retrenchment

The MPD and FMI authorities did not take this lying down. They countered with the usual charges: skeptics were in denial over child abuse, they were misogynists, they were right-wingers, they were preventing survivors from healing. In the third edition of *The Courage to Heal*, Bass and Davis try to do salvage work. If you discover that part of your abuse story isn't true, they say, that doesn't mean that the other parts aren't true. If you now doubt that you suffered sexual abuse, "focus on healing from the emotional abuse." Whatever, as long as you don't give up claiming that you were abused.[1]

Putnam, ever humane, speculated that the cause of MPD skepticism must be anxiety: "One wonders what it is that critics fear most—MPD per se, or what it says about the human condition." Others felt that MPD doubters must have psychological problems. They were displacing rage; they were dissociating, hallucinating. They were dupes of the conspiracy; they *were* the conspiracy. "The 'False Memory Syndrome' is a sham invented by pedophiles and sex abusers for the media," wrote psychiatrist Robert B. Rockwell in the *Journal of Psychohistory* in 1994. (Four years later, after an investigation of his treatment of patients for cult abuse, the state of New York suspended Rockwell's license to practice medicine.) Colin Ross suggested a financial motive: "Some expert witnesses on false memory . . . probably have made millions of dollars in fees." (He neglected to mention that he himself has appeared repeatedly as an expert witness in RM cases. Pendergrast reports that in 1995 Ross's fee was $5,000 per day, plus expenses.) As for the retractors, Ross offered the theory that they were making a symbolic substitution of memories for semen: the therapist, accused of implanting memories, "has been identified with the incest perpetrator, who implanted semen in his daughter." "Therefore," he continued, "therapists should be able to launch false memory suits against patients, lawyers, and background organizations suing them. I am considering doing so."[2]

These fighting words are from Ross's "President's Message" to the members of the ISSMP&D in 1994. The following year, however, the "President's Message" was quite different. "I refuse to be intimidated into not confronting the increasing troubles in our field," wrote Nancy Hornstein, Ross's successor as head of the organization. The troubles, she said, had to do with therapists' "presupposing that clients' reports or 'memories' are in accordance with fact." (Note the quotation marks on "memories.") She made a number of recommendations—above all, that therapists should stay neutral regarding the truth of the patient's memories and that they should not dwell on the abreaction of those memories. She ended by asking her colleagues to remember Hippocrates' command to physicians: "Do no harm."[3]

As is obvious from the MPD literature of the 1990s, it was Hornstein's letter, not Ross's, that reflected the growing sentiment of the field. MPD therapists at last realized that harm had been done—or in any case that their colleagues were being sued. They now acknowledged that at least in some cases the disorder seemed to have been created through therapy. Many of them tried to blame this on a lunatic fringe: kooks, zealots, graduates of weekend workshops. But since prominent experts in the field—Braun, Ross, Kluft, all of them MDs—were among the people facing lawsuits, such an argument became increasingly hard to make. Also, it was clear that even in the disasters produced by therapists of lesser standing, the teachings of the experts were at work. Humenansky, when asked under oath where she learned the techniques she used in the case of Elizabeth Carlson, replied that she had gotten them from Colin Ross, Bennett Braun, and Frank Putnam.

≫ ≪

Damage control now began. First, the name of the disorder was changed. In 1994, in the fourth edition of *DSM*, multiple personality disorder emerged unglamorously rechristened as "dissociative identity disorder," or DID. The Stanford psychiatrist David Spiegel, who headed the dissociative disorders work group for the *DSM* revision, explained to me the reasons for the change: "We wanted to emphasize that the critical problem was the failure of integration, rather than the proliferation of personalities. Also, we wanted this condition to be regarded like any other mental disorder, and not like some weird, far-out, cultlike thing." In other words, he wanted it cleansed of the unfortunate associations it had acquired. (Compare "colored" to "negroes" to "blacks" to "African Americans.") He and his colleagues also no doubt wanted the press off MPD's back. In the words of George Ganaway, "Geraldo's ratings would have been a lot lower if *TV Guide* had said, 'Today Geraldo is going to interview someone with dissociative identity disorder.'"[4] Other new words followed. In 1995 the ISSMP&D dropped the offending "MP" and became just the International Society for the Study of Dissociation (ISSD). "Recovered memory" became "delayed recall." "Satanic ritual abuse" became "ritual abuse" or "sadistic abuse."

It was like a presidential campaign: everyone moved to the center. Colin Ross began appearing as an expert witness not just for defendants, but for plaintiffs too, in negligence suits. Where in his 1989 textbook he had written that "three quarters of MPD patients can be treated to integration in less than 2½ years," now, in his 1997 revision of the book, he changed the sentence to read that "three quarters of *Kluft's* DID patients were treated to integration in less than 2½ years." (Italics mine.) Kluft said it, not Ross. But the direction in which the wind was blowing could best be judged from a one-word change in Ross's book. In the 1989 edition he had said that MPD "is not an iatrogenic artifact." In the 1997 edition he said that the disorder "is not solely an iatrogenic artifact." Ross also used the opportunity of the revision to distance himself from Braun, who at that moment was facing the scandalous Shanley and Burgus lawsuits. Whereas in the 1989 book he described Braun as having founded "the world's leading Dissociative Disorders unit," now Braun had merely founded "the world's first Dissociative Disorders unit." Braun, he pointed out in the new edition, was no longer chairing the annual meetings of the ISSD, as he had from 1984 to 1994. Indeed, the meetings had been moved out of Braun's city, Chicago—lest, presumably, they catch his germs. Ross acknowledged "the great debt the field owes Dr. Braun."[5] Good luck, Dr. Braun!

But these maneuverings were minor compared with the changes in technique now recommended by Ross and other MPD authorities. As noted, Hornstein, in her "President's Message," made two main proposals: first, that therapists not endorse the patient's abuse memories, but remain neutral; second, that MPD therapy not dwell on the abreaction of those memories. It is no coincidence that of all the aspects of MPD therapy, abuse memories were the focus of both these recommendations—they were the focus of the lawsuits. The field endorsed the changes. Christine Curtois, who in her 1988 *Healing the Incest Wound* had stated unequivocally that "the therapist must make explicit that the survivor's story is believed," now wrote that the therapist might "never know if real abuse occurred" and must therefore neither believe nor disbelieve.[6] Bennett Braun too called for neutrality: he now stated that any abuse story, to be believed, had to have corroboration.[7] (Where was his corroboration when he plied the Burgus boys, aged four and five, for memories of their participation in SRA massacres?) As for abreaction, which before had been central to MPD therapy, experts now disavowed it. In 1989 Colin Ross wrote that in MPD treatment "the therapist should be uncomfortable if intense abreactions are not occurring." In 1997 he wrote that when patients in his unit abreacted he told them that this was "acting out, hurtful to the other patients, evidence that the person is not serious about recovery, and grounds for negative countertransference." (In other words, the therapist would get angry at them.) He also warned them that repeated abreactions were grounds for transfer to the "general adult unit," the place with the schizophrenics.[8]

But that was not all they backed off from. Putnam, who in his book had taught therapists how to get hypnotized patients to search their minds for "painful or frightening experiences," now warned against "blind probing for suspected trauma." Hypnosis too began losing its friends. Kluft, who in 1982 had described using hypnosis to gather "historical information" in sixty-seven out of a group of seventy patients, now said that his use of hypnosis to recover memory was "fairly infrequent." D. Corydon Hammond, who in his 1990 textbook on hypnosis had taught therapists how to manipulate hypnotized patients—how to create a "yes-set," how to use salesmen's "foot-in-the-door technique"—now cautioned against leading the patient. "It is vitally important for the therapist to seek to create neutral expectations before hypnotic exploration," he wrote. (Compare, in his textbook: "In hypnosis it is vitally important to create a sense of positive expectancy in the patient.")[9]

Even alters, the very hallmark of MPD, started getting the cold shoulder. David Spiegel told me that though a patient may believe she has alternate personalities, that doesn't mean that the therapist believes her—"any more than you believe a schizophrenic when she says she's the Virgin Mary. You believe the experience but not necessarily the metaphor." He does address his patients' alters, he says, but he calls them "the Mary Ellen part of yourself" rather than "Mary Ellen." Other therapists don't even want to hear about the Mary Ellen part of yourself. In one of the numerous damage-control books that have come out since the RM/MPD scandals, Seth Segall of Yale writes a judicious essay in which he speaks repeatedly of the MPD patient's "ego states." One has to read for a few paragraphs before one realizes that these "ego states" are the things that were once known as alters. The "child ego state," says Segall, is simply part of the patient and should be treated no differently from the patient.[10] No more talking to teddy bears.

But if the MPD therapists are throwing out their old techniques, what are their new techniques? What is MPD treatment today? According to the official "Guidelines for Treating Dissociative Identity Disorder" published by the ISSD in 1997, most MPD treaters employ a "psychodynamically aware psychotherapy" aimed at building ego strength. The patient is addressed as a "whole person," a "single person," "not a collection of separate people sharing the same body." Abreactions are deemphasized. Hypnosis, when used, is aimed primarily at "calming, soothing, containment, and ego strengthening." It is also used to "help patients terminate spontaneous flashbacks." (No mention here that its main use, before, was to *induce* flashbacks.) Informed consent is required for hypnosis. "Exclusive focus on past traumatic material to the exclusion of contemporary issues" is discouraged. On the accuracy of patients' trauma memories, the therapist should take "a respectful neutral stance."[11] If this is in fact what MPD therapists are now doing, then they are offering a mild, conservative treatment far distant from what was known as MPD therapy in the 1980s. Some current writers act as if they barely recognized the old MPD therapy. "We never did it," the general message goes, "and let's not do it any more."

For any clinician unmoved by the new treatment recommendations, the damage-control books contain vivid discussions of the legal problems that may ensue. "Any clinical case is potentially a forensic case," write Kenneth Pope and Laura Brown in their 1996 *Recovered Memories of Abuse*, and they offer therapists a preview of what a forensic case can be like. They give them a list of fifty-seven questions they might be asked under cross-examination, and they quote various attorneys on the experience of cross-examination: how witnesses sweat and twitch, how "burning questions" are hurled at them.[12] The authors even provide a sample subpoena! These, they say, are the things readers might think about if they want to continue doing recovered-memory therapy.

Old-style RM and MPD therapy is no doubt still going on. As recently as 1995 the Poole group's survey of doctoral-level therapists in the United States found that more than one-fourth used hypnosis to help clients recover memories of childhood sexual abuse. If that figure is representative of American psychotherapy in general—in fact, it is probably low (doctoral-level therapists would probably be more cautious than others)—it translates into tens of thousands of clinicians. Not all of them will have changed their ways in just a few years.[13]

Actually, old-fashioned MPD therapy may still be going on in the offices of the reformed. Here, for example, is Colin Ross, in his 1994 casebook, giving us an example of how he does *not* use hypnosis and does *not* give suggestions for multiplicity. The patient, Mary, is dissociative; she has "blank spells."

> I decided not to ask about other people inside at all, but instead . . . I carried out a simple relaxation exercise, asking her to close her eyes, relax, and feel her body becoming warm and comfortable. . . . I then asked to speak to a part of the mind that remembers what happens during the blank spells. I suggested that it would be just like when Mary has a blank spell out in the world: Mary would be like she had gone inside, like she had gone to sleep, and another part of the mind would be here— awake, eyes open, and able to talk with us. . . . I did not say that this other part of the mind would be personified, feel like a separate person, or have a different name.[14]

Surprise! All unbidden, another part of the mind emerged. Not having been warned that she should have a different name, she introduced herself as Mary. (Ross called her "the second Mary.") A week later he repeated the procedure and got "Eleanor," and the job was done.

※ ※

Nevertheless, it is clear that the MPD movement is dying. The more the therapists worry about lawsuits, the more they will show neutrality on the subject of the patient's abuse memories, and the more they stay neutral, the fewer such memories they will hear. When, in the face of a story of sexual assault, the therapist just says, "Hmmm, go on," this will affect the future production of such stories very differently from the therapist's saying, "How terrible! And then what did he do?" The cycle of mutual reinforcement—patient gratifying therapist with theory-confirming abuse stories, therapist gratifying patient with attention and sympathy—will be broken. At the same time, hypnosis, that crucial memory-fetcher of MPD, will be used much less. As noted, some malpractice policies no longer cover it.

Finally, what neutrality and the discouragement of hypnosis do not accomplish, the current demand for "informed consent" will. An insurance executive specializing in mental-health malpractice told me that he advises his clients as follows: informed consent for any therapy involving recovered memory must include, first, telling the patient about the current controversy over RM and, second, warning her that she will not be able to go to court alleging the truth of whatever memories they uncover. As he concedes, this will throw cold water over any intent to recover memories, and no doubt over the patient–therapist relationship as well. The alternative is not to do RM therapy, and that is the path that most therapists are probably choosing, for abuse accusations seem to be declining precipitously. In a 1999 issue of the *False Memory Syndrome Foundation Newsletter* Pamela Freyd reported that calls to the foundation from newly accused families were "now no more than a trickle."[15]

❧ ❦

Many therapists object to this backpedaling. "It's like they've taken us hostage," one therapist told *Philadelphia* magazine. Others feel they are being forced to betray their patients. In a 1995 essay, psychoanalyst Sue Grand describes how she reacted when a patient of hers voiced a suspicion that she had been a victim of incest. Instead of just worrying about the patient, Grand began worrying about herself as well:

> I will be implicated. Financially ruined, professionally humiliated. I am a little girl, terrorized, with a shameful secret. Even as she weeps, she does not yet know but who has lost me. I hear the howls of judicial accusation: Have I suggested this? How can I demonstrate that I haven't? Should I start taping to protect myself, and how to explain this to the patient? . . . Suddenly I feel I must demonstrate to the patient that these [incest] images may be more symbolic than literal.[16]

Grand thinks she betrayed this patient, but did she? Even without the legal problem, recent memory research, together with the sheer amount of social contagion on the subject of abuse, suggests that it was not a bad idea to tell the patient that her images might be more symbolic than literal. And what if this patient *was* abused, and never finds out? Is it worse for her to have an unexplored true abuse history than for other women to have endlessly explored and fervently embraced false abuse histories? Therapists are going to have to err in one direction or the other.

For now, it's the false memories they're worried about. The number of new diagnoses of MPD seems to be dropping year by year. The dissociative disorders units are closing. (Reportedly, about half the DD units in the United States have shut their doors in the last five or six years.) MPD inpatients are being sent to the general adult units, where, with their multiplicity unreinforced by special treatment, or by day-to-day life in a community of multiples, they are probably going home a lot sooner. Satanic ritual abuse claims are far rarer now than in the 1980s.

With these supports removed, the ISSD has entered what its 1999 president, Peter Barach, calls a "crisis." Between 1993 and 1998 the organization lost almost half its members, about fifteen hundred people. In 1998, the society's journal, *Dissociation*, ceased publication. By 1999, staff was being let go. The organization offered to integrate itself into the International Society for Traumatic Stress Studies, a group to which a number of ISSD members, interested in trauma but no longer interested in MPD, had switched their allegiance. "Unfortunately," Barach reports, "the ISTSS did not accept the proposal."[17] Many people today want no part of multiple personality disorder.

That includes leading authors of *DSM-IV*. In a 1998 book called *Your Mental Health*, a "layman's guide" to the diagnostic manual, Allen Frances, head of the *DSM-IV* task force, and Michael First, the editor of *DSM-IV*, write that while they do not deny the existence of rare cases of MPD, MPD therapy "may do more harm than good. . . . We would recommend avoiding any treatment that seeks to discover new personalities or to uncover past traumas." Indeed, the authors recommend against trusting an MPD diagnosis: "A good rule of thumb is that any condition that has become a favorite with Hollywood, Oprah, and checkout-counter newspapers and magazines stands a great chance of being wildly overdiagnosed. . . . If you are wondering whether you qualify for this diagnosis, it is a very good bet that you almost surely do not."[18] One wonders whether MPD, or DID, will qualify as a primary-level diagnosis in the next edition of *DSM*.

9

The Effects

In the MPD retrenchment, it is hard to tell whether the principal cause was the lawsuits or medical cost-cutting, for the two happened at the same time. Cost-cutting is usually blamed for the closing of the DD units. Without doubt, it was also a factor in the decrease of MPD diagnoses. To quote Michael Simpson, "One of the characteristics of MPD is that it occurs principally in the context of the availability of lengthy psychodynamic psychotherapy affordable by the patient."[1] That context has vanished. Ten years ago my health insurance covered 80 percent of the costs of psychotherapy after a deductible of $1,000, with the number of sessions per week to be determined between the therapist and the insurance company. Today my plan, after a deductible of $750, pays for 50 percent of twenty sessions per year, period. Recall that classic MPD therapy, at least as described by Putnam, required two to three extended sessions (one and a half hours) per week.[2] That is the equivalent of *one hundred eighty* sessions per year. At medium New York rates, this would cost $18,000 per year, of which, with my insurance, I would be paying $17,000 per year—for three to five years, according to Putnam. I could not afford to be a multiple.

Of course, a great deal of RM and MPD therapy was paid for by the government rather than by private insurers. But that support too is being cut back. In 1997 the crime victims' compensation program in the state of Washington, the same state that first extended its statutes of limitations to allow for recovered memory, declared that it would no longer pay for therapies focusing on repressed memories. (Investigators had found that the people receiving such therapy were getting worse, not better.) In ten or twenty years, MPD will probably be a rare disorder again.

※ ※

The MPD movement will not die, however, without leaving its mark on psychotherapy. The whole trend in psychological treatment in the last twenty years has been away from the long-term, Freud-based, childhood-examining "insight" therapy of yesteryear and toward drug treatment and/or short-term (ten- to twenty-session) "cognitive-behavioral" therapy, in which patients address their present-day problems. This change has been hard on many therapists. They went into the profession because they were interested in the deeper reaches of the mind; they studied for years how to explore those territories; then they graduated into a field that was about Prozac and assertiveness training. The life they intended to lead was no longer there, nor was the income they intended to earn. (Insofar as the field was about drugs, non-MD therapists were shut out altogether. Only physicians can prescribe drugs.) To make matters worse, the field had expanded. From 1959 to 1989, membership in the American Psychological Association grew by a factor of *sixteen*. That is not to mention the psychiatric social workers, the psychiatric nurses, the various unlicensed counselors. (In most states, no license whatsoever is required in order to advertise oneself as a psychotherapist.) Their numbers had risen even faster.

The growth of the field unquestionably contributed to the RM/MPD movement. For one thing, most of the new entrants were female. (The majority of American psychotherapists are now women.) As psychotherapy became feminized, there was a shift from the old, Freudian, interpretive approach, where the therapist told the patient what really happened in her life—and where, as we saw, incest memories were decoded as oedipal fantasies—to a new, empathic, egalitarian treatment in which the therapist was much more likely to take the patient's recollections at face value. Hence, in part, recovered memory therapy.

But women aside, MPD provided new business for a hard-up profession. A widespread mental disorder that had no accepted drug treatment and that required three to five years of two or three extended sessions per week—for those seeking to revive insight therapy, this was the answer to a prayer. Actually, many MPD claims were not billed as MPD. Even in the eighties, this diagnosis was likely to result in phone calls from the insurance company. So the bills were sent in with a different diagnosis (often depression) at the same time that, in the therapist's mind, the "true diagnosis of MPD legitimized the intensive treatment. For a large number of insurers, the mere fact of an abuse claim—forget the diagnosis—justified extended therapy, in the course of which, as the trauma memories were probed hour after hour, MPD might just develop. In the words of Christopher Barden, a psychologist–attorney who helped win the landmark decisions in the Elizabeth Carlson, Vynette Hamanne, and Patricia Burgus cases, recovered memory could "turn a $2000 eating disorder patient into a $200,000 multiple personality disorder."[3] Two hundred thousand may be low. Patricia Burgus's MPD cost $1 million; Mary Shanley's, $2 million.

Much of this happened, furthermore, before the advent of managed care. Once that occurred, with therapists in some states averaging a 50 percent loss of income, the need for MPD became all the greater. Jack Leggett, a clinical psychologist who has worked for various managed care companies, explains the situation: "If you're a psychotherapist, and someone presents with a chemical dependency, and I'm the managed-care reviewer, I'm going to want him detoxed and referred to a structured alcohol treatment program. I'm not going to leave him in weekly psychotherapy with you."[4] This state of affairs may help to explain such things as "phenocopy MPD," where the patients just *look* like alcoholics—or schizophrenics or transvestites or whatever—but they're really multiples.

The market pressure in outpatient therapy was accompanied by a parallel crisis in the mental hospitals. Between 1984 and 1988, under Reagan and deregulation, the number of private psychiatric hospitals in the United States more than doubled. But at the same time that their number was growing, so were two trends that would work against psychiatric hospitalization: drug therapy and medical cost-cutting. By the late 1980s, the new for-profit mental hospitals were looking at thousands of empty beds. In response, many of them began what Joe Sharkey, in his 1994 book *Bedlam*, calls "guerrilla marketing."[5] They got rid of their doctor-directors and hired business executives. They set up networks of bounty hunters—social workers, school counselors, probation officers, hotline workers, even the clergy—to refer people to their facilities. They sent pizzas to police stations. Once they got an adult patient, they suggested that his or her children also come in for "evaluation"—a procedure that often resulted in the children's being hospitalized. (Between 1980 and 1987, Sharkey reports, the number of Americans aged ten to nineteen who spent time in psychiatric hospitals increased by 43 percent.) The hospitals offered princely retainers to psychotherapists who provided the right diagnoses— diagnoses that would keep patients in the hospital until the insurance allowance for that coverage period ran out, and justify their return once a new coverage period started.

Multiple personality disorder fit beautifully into this system. If the MP's need for several years of intensive psychotherapy answered the prayers of outpatient clinicians, her "suicidality," typically increasing as her therapy continued, filled the inpatient side of the bill. Suicidal patients need to be hospitalized. Recall that Mary Shanley was in the hospital for two years, Patricia Burgus for three, and that their children were hospitalized as well. A 1995 article in the *Houston Press* lists the various families—mothers and children (never the fathers, it seems)—that Judith Peterson hospitalized at Spring Shadows Glen in Houston once she became head of its dissociative disorders unit in 1990.[6] In the early 1990s, that unit was bringing in $15,600 a day, a fact that may well have discouraged staff inquiries into what was going on in Peterson's MPD therapy.

Even when the patient's hospitalization allowance ran out, arrangements could be made. In *Victims of Memory*, Pendergrast tells the story of Christy Steck, one of Peterson's patients at Spring Shadows Glen. When Steck was notified by her insurance company that her hospitalization coverage was almost exhausted, Peterson's colleague Bennett Braun flew down from Chicago, evaluated Steck, and wrote a report describing her as a "catastrophic case." This enabled her, via a special clause in her policy, to remain in the hospital and go on exploring her many alters—including Tyrant, Tricia, Whore, and Fucking Bitch with Judith Peterson.[7] According to the indictment in the Spring Shadows Glen case, the hospital also kept track of whether certain patients were paying their insurance premiums, and if the patient could not pay, the hospital did, thus ensuring its ability to go on collecting from the insurance company.

Like so many other supports of RM/MPD therapy, this system fell apart in the early 1990s. Managed care came in. Furthermore, the state and federal governments began investigating the private psychiatric hospital corporations. Federal agents walked into the hospitals and walked out with boxloads of medical records. In the ensuing lawsuits, hospital executives, all the while claiming that their accusers were in denial over the American public's need for psychiatric hospitalization, were forced to settle for vast sums. In 1993, National Medical Enterprises, one of the four leaders of the field, agreed to pay $125 million. Charter Medical Corporation, another giant of the industry, ended up in bankruptcy. (It was back in business the following year.)

These government investigations should be kept in mind apropos of the fantastic cult theories, implicating the government, that were propagated by Braun, Ross, Hammond, and others in the early 1990s. Ross was an employee of Charter Medical Corporation. Judith Peterson's DD unit was closed down by the state of Texas in

1993. (Indeed, the hospital itself closed and then reopened under a new owner and a new name, Memorial Spring Shadows Glen.) Peterson doesn't blame the government, though. In a 1993 interview with the *Houston Chronicle* she offered the theory that the culprit was organized crime. "I think organized crime could use people in child prostitution and drug running and then, through memory layering, disguise or cover it," she explained. In a 1995 deposition she said she believed that organized crime operatives were wearing masks designed to look like her face in order to confuse and traumatize patients.[8]

The MPD movement, Christopher Barden says flatly, was at least in part an effort by certain therapists to increase their "market share." Higher motives were no doubt operating as well, for example, the desire, in the face of drug treatment and cognitive-behavioral techniques, to make psychotherapy interesting again. "If someone comes into my office," says Jack Leggett, "and it's kind of a depression and I'm kind of working through their life, it's not as exciting as if I'm in a life-and-death struggle with devil personalities and hooker personalities and little-crying-child personalities."[9]

The political climate of the 1980s should also be taken into account. In a time of Republican ascendancy, with widespread calls for no more entitlements, no more excuses, a claim of childhood sexual abuse might have seemed to some beleaguered people the untrumpable card. (Even today, RM skeptics are far more likely to question the truth of an abuse claim than to say, "Get over it.") For clinicians too, and especially for feminist clinicians, the RM/MPD movement must have looked like a warm corner in an increasingly cold society. Nevertheless, these considerations were not unaccompanied by financial benefits.

≫ ≪

So MPD was, in part, an attempt to rescue insight therapy. And it did the opposite; it covered insight therapy with shame, highlighting all of its long-standing problems, above all its problems with

truth. When critics of MPD therapy say that the memories involved
are not retrieved but rather created, in a collaboration between
patient and therapist, they are pointing to something that has been
part of insight therapy at least since Freud. Nor are therapists ignorant of this. They call it "narrative truth." In the words of psychologist G. A. Bonanno, "The task of the therapist . . . is not to help
the patients retrieve lost memories (historical truth) but to foster
the development of a more advanced conceptual understanding in
which to perceive and revise their life stories (narrative truth)."[10]
This system chugged along quietly as long as the memories were
about toilet training or sibling rivalry, and as long as incest stories,
if they came up, were taken as symbolic, in keeping with Freud's
revision of his seduction theory. But once therapists decided that
Freud was right the first time—that a vast number of women really
had been sexually assaulted by their fathers—and once those
women accused their fathers, indeed sued them, narrative truth was
not OK any more. One needed historical truth.

Many therapists counseled their patients strongly against suing
their alleged abusers, even against confronting them.[11] The reasons
they give for this vary. Some speak of the inevitable damage to the
patient's relationship with her family. Others point to the emotional
stress of a lawsuit. Let me propose another reason: a lawsuit might
reveal the insubstantiality of the abuse memories that were the
RM/MPD therapists' stock-in-trade. Many MPD-treaters no more
wanted their clients' abuse memories exposed to legal testing than
the Catholic clergy wanted the Shroud of Turin exposed to carbon-
14 testing. And in large measure, they have had their way. In the
Poole group's 1995 survey of therapists, only 6 percent of patients
who had retrieved memories of childhood sexual abuse had taken
legal action.

But some therapists, particularly feminists, did not approve of
this policy. Their faith was stronger; they *believed* their patients' stories. They also believed in the criminal justice system, and they rea-
soned that child-molesting was not going to stop until the guilty

were accused and punished—an argument that seems unassailable. Unfortunately, many of these therapists also encouraged women to construct abuse claims on the flimsiest of foundations. In the words of *The Courage to Heal*, "To say 'I was abused,' you don't need the kind of proof that would stand up in a court of law." This no doubt emboldened many people, who then found out, once they arrived in a court of law, that in fact they did need the kind of evidence that would hold up in a court of law. According to a legal survey by the False Memory Syndrome Foundation, only a third of the RM lawsuits ("rememberer" suing alleged abuser) concluded between 1989 and 1996 were won by the plaintiff or settled out of court. Almost half were dismissed.[12] Many got a lot of press, and the public found out what was going on in RM therapy.

And what did the therapists now say? That they had done nothing wrong—that though, in keeping with RM orthodoxy, they had sought and supported these memories, they didn't know whether the patients' recall was accurate, and it wasn't their job to know. They were therapists, not police officers. They dealt with narrative truth, not historical truth.

The *Frontline* documentary "Divided Memories" tells the story of a young woman, "Ann Norris" (twenty-seven alters), who at the time of the show was suing her parents and grandparents. According to her therapist, Ann remembered in the course of treatment that she had been born into a cult and subjected to vicious abuse—that, for example, her mother had inserted spiders, wires, and a broomstick into her vagina, had attached electrodes to her genitals, had tortured her sexually with tools from the hardware store. The interviewers spoke to Ann's father, who, close to tears, called the charges an "absurdity." Ann's childhood medical records, he said, showed no evidence of abuse, and her school records for the period of her putative cult tortures showed perfect attendance.

The interviewers then asked Ann's therapist, Douglas Sawin of Costa Mesa, California, whether her $20 million suit, which he was supporting, might be founded on a delusion. "We all live in a delusion," he replied. "Do any of us know the truth?" he asked. He added that in legal depositions (Ann's suit was apparently not the first to issue from his office) he was frequently asked how he knew the patient's story was true: "And I say, 'I don't care if it's true. What's important to me is that I hear the child's truth, the patient's truth. . . . What actually happened is irrelevant. It doesn't matter.'" Sawin is not the only epistemologist out there. Colin Ross writes, "I have worked with Satanic ritual abuse memories which were impossible for me to believe, and with patients reporting mind control, abduction, child sacrifice, paedophilia, and sophisticated use of hypnosis who I judged could be giving me historical facts. In the majority of cases, I am not sure one way or the other, but do not worry about it much." In any case, he does not question the patient's story. "Expressing doubt damages the treatment alliance," he says.[13]

Is there any other line of work, outside the criminal professions, in which experts routinely hear firsthand reports of child-molesting and murder and do not worry whether they are true? What if some of them *are* true? There are cases in Ross's writings, and also in *The Courage to Heal*, that sound plausible, yet no one ever seems to have called the police. In July 1993 a woman named Susan Mroczynski appeared on CNN's *Larry King Live* asserting that she had seen hundreds of people murdered by the cult she belonged to and that she had participated in many of the murders. Why was she not in police custody? Because, one might say, nobody believed her. But all the people who called in to the show did believe her. (They wanted to know how they could tell if they were victims of satanic ritual abuse, and how to get a good SRA therapist.) What, then, did the callers think of the criminal justice system? In its indifference to the truth of abuse claims, RM therapy has probably been a substantial contributor to the paranoia that has swept American politics in the last twenty years.

Those who, hearing Mroczynski's story, did not feel that the country was endangered by satanic cults must have felt that it was endangered by RM/MPD therapy, a profession that had unmoored itself from truth in what seemed to be an effort to stay in business—a profession, furthermore, that while righteously accusing its critics of protecting pedophiles, was arranging, via its discouragement of lawsuits, for alleged pedophiles to go unchallenged. Or that's what the therapists were doing if they believed their patients' accounts. If they did not believe those accounts, then they were arranging for thousands of women to go through their lives falsely believing that they had been raped as children. Small wonder that Herbert Spiegel calls MPD therapy a "racket."[14]

❧ ❧

Of course, some people regard all long-term psychotherapy as a racket. For decades now, Freud and his legacy have been under attack. The MPD establishment, as noted, are among his harshest critics, because he abandoned the seduction theory and because psychoanalysis eclipsed MPD. But as Ian Hacking has pointed out, their objections to him were probably exacerbated by a knowledge of their debt to him. Most of the coercive techniques of MPD therapy come warmly recommended in Freud's writings. If patients claim not to have the memory the therapist is looking for, he wrote, "We must not believe what they say, we must always assume, and tell them, too, that they have kept something back. . . . We must insist on this, we must repeat the pressure and represent ourselves as infallible, till at last we are really told something." If the patient gives up and produces something, but not quite what the therapist wants, "We tell our patient that this explains nothing, but that behind it there must be hidden a more significant, earlier experience." If the patient supplies what is wanted but then later says the therapist put it in his head, "I remain unshakably firm. I . . . explain to the patient that [these distinctions] are only forms of his resistance." I have taken the above quotations from Frederick Crews's book *The Memory Wars*, which makes the point that our society's continuing acceptance of Freud's ideas helped lay the groundwork for the RM scandal. The "vulgar pseudoscience of recovered memory," Crews writes, "rests in appreciable measure on the respectable and entrenched pseudoscience of psychoanalysis."[15]

Some therapists have tried very hard to shield Freud from tarring with the RM/MPD brush. Recovered-memory therapy, writes George Ganaway, is simply a "kidnapping" of Freud, a use of his "earliest and least sophisticated psychoanalytic theories" in a way that "trivializes the complexity of the human mind," the very complexity that he spent his later years exploring. Janice Haaken, of Portland State University, has argued that Freud, early in his career, turned his back on the concept of dissociation, where memory was simply walled off and could be recovered whole—the idea, in other words, at the bottom of RM therapy—in favor of the richer concept of repression, in which the mind continually worked on the memory, using it, transforming it. If the RM therapists had read the mature Freud, these critics suggest, they would never have made the mistakes they made.[16]

In fact, Freudian theory did father RM/MPD therapy. That therapy's most basic ideas—that the cause of people's problems is a childhood sexual secret, that the secret has been driven from consciousness, that it thereupon creates symptoms, that to relieve the symptoms the secret must be revealed, and that this process should be the focus of treatment—are Freud's most basic ideas. (It should not be forgotten that Cornelia Wilbur, whose handling of Sybil became the model for MPD therapy, was an orthodox Freudian.) Freud too earned his living helping people spin life stories that had no known basis in fact. He too cut his theory to fit his convenience.

Many reasons have been proposed for Freud's abandonment of the seduction theory. Let me suggest another one: given that theory, his job would have been rendered morally impossible. As long as he went on asserting that his patients' psychological disorders were caused by childhood molestation, and that this crime was a routine feature of middle-class domestic life in Vienna, he could not have sat in his office doing what he wanted to do. He would have had to go to the police. So, having once lumped his patients' sex stories together and called them child abuse, he changed his mind. He lumped his patients' sex stories together and called them fantasy. In the process, as feminist writers have pointed out, he gave society an excuse to ignore true cases of child-molesting for the better part of a century.

≫ ≪

Yet if RM/MPD therapy is descended from Freud, so are the other insight therapies, most of them drastically modified since Freud's day (less intensive, less authoritarian, less sex-crazed, less fixated on the past), that are going on across this land—with, in many cases, decent-minded professionals trying to help people with hard problems that they cannot discuss with anyone else. Even cognitive-behavioral therapy, in its cognitive component, can trace its origins to Freud. Such treatments should not be condemned because they share a common source with RM/MPD therapy.

Still, it is true that the insight therapies have little grounding in science, that they deal in "narrative truth," that they depend on an emotional bond between an unhappy, help-seeking patient and a therapist in a position of considerable power. Thus, in the hands of the wrong people, they are vulnerable to the abuses that created the recovered-memory and MPD epidemics. For this reason, they are now more suspect than they have ever been. In 1995, Christopher Barden began circulating to the federal and state legislatures a proposal for a new law, the "Truth and Responsibility in Mental Health Practices Act." A key sentence reads: "No tax or tax exempt moneys may be used for any form of health care treatment, including any form of psychotherapy, that has not been proven safe and effective by rigorous, valid and reliable scientific investigations and accepted as safe and effective by a substantial majority of the relevant scientific community."[17] The law would also include requirements for informed consent. Barden's letter of proposal is signed not just by him but by a number of the most respected psychologists and psychiatrists in the country.

Note, in the proposed law, the words "tax exempt": this statute would exclude coverage of such therapies not only by public programs but also by private insurers, since the insured write off the cost of health insurance. But the critical words are "rigorous, valid and reliable scientific investigations." Numerous forms of insight therapy have not been proven safe and effective by such means, nor are they likely to be. As with MPD therapy, many of their tenets therapy are non-falsifiable; they can't be scientifically tested. In Barden's view, this means that such therapies have no right to claim insurance-coverage parity with medical treatments, which are scientifically testable. "All we are saying," Barden summarizes, "is that if there is no reliable evidence that this procedure helps, the taxpayers should not get the bill for it. If these therapists want to set up booths outside the astrology stores, that's fine. But there is no reason why a farmer in Kansas should go to work at four in the morning to pay them."[18]

Needless to say, many therapists oppose the so-called Barden bill. "It's a know-nothing assault on the enterprise of psychotherapy," says David Spiegel. According to Ofshe and Watters, the American Psychological Association in 1995 set aside almost a million dollars to fight such legislation. That organization should have considered earlier what the results of RM/MPD therapy would be. Of all the most important professional organizations concerned with this scandal, the American Psychological Association has been the slowest and weakest in pointing out the abuses involved. As late as 1995, when the RM movement was backed to the wall, the association published a paper, "Questions and Answers About Memories of Childhood Abuse," in which it came down firmly on both sides of the issue. "A competent psychologist is likely to acknowledge that current knowledge does not allow the definite conclusion that a memory is real or false without other corroborating evidence," says the paper.[19] Clearly, the sentence that someone proposed to the committee was, "A memory cannot be judged true or false without corroborating evidence"—an assertion supported by reams of scientific literature. But lest any of the members of APA feel that this was inconsistent with their practice, the qualifiers were laid on—"*likely* to acknowledge," "*current* knowledge," "*definite* conclusion," and best of all, "*other* corroborating evidence" (all italics mine), as if the memory itself constituted corroborating evidence—with the result that the point is more or less lost among the loopholes.

Actually, a number of treatment-outcome studies have found that for many neurotic-level problems insight therapy is about as effective as drug or cognitive-behavioral therapy. The catch is that insight therapy is much more expensive than those other treatments. Partisans of insight therapy would say that it's worth it—that what they need is to talk about their lives (including their past), not take a pill or, as in cognitive-behavioral therapy, revise their "self-statements." Opponents would say fine, as long as the patients pay for it with their own money—in which case insight therapy will go back to being what it was before the sixties, a luxury for the rich. In some measure that is what it is now, just as a result of medical cost-cutting.

≫ ≪

If RM/MPD treatment damaged the reputation of psychotherapy, it also discredited the child protection movement, the very thing that, aside from patients, it was supposed to serve.[20] With Bass and Davis including every pat on the fanny under child-molesting, the claims of widespread abuse came to seem absurd—"abuse excuse"—and as a result genuine cases were cast into doubt as well. "When everything is child abuse, nothing is," as Wendy Kaminer has put it.[21]

It should also be kept in mind that some genuine claims probably sound absurd already. Either the woman has watched too much TV or she has read the RM/MPD literature, which is full of fantastic tales. In any case, by the time she tells her story, the single abuser has become twenty abusers, with horns. (This is not to speak of how the tale will be elaborated once she begins therapy.) By accepting such stories, the MPD therapists made it that much more likely not only that the public would ultimately reject the whole abuse epidemic but that, in cases such as this, the woman would have no hope of relocating something like the truth; she would never know what happened to her. Indeed, such a woman might have trouble, today, finding someone to treat her. As a result of the RM/MPD lawsuits, therapists are now being advised in "risk management" workshops not to take on dissociative patients. In other words, the therapeutic movement that was aimed at abuse survivors is resulting in the abandonment of abuse survivors.

At the same time, the RM/MPD movement has substantially detoxified childhood sexual abuse. The inflated statistics, to begin with, make abuse seem normal: if one-third of the women who get up in the morning and wash their faces and go to work were molested as children, then how damaging can that experience be? Furthermore, the subject of child abuse—once taboo, not to be spoken of—is now all around us, seeping into our pores, getting us used to it. It fills our magazines, our movies, our books, and not just the lowbrow literature. Consider, in just the past few years, Jane Smiley's *A Thousand Acres*, A. M. Homes's *The End of Alice*, Margaret Atwood's *The Robber Bride*, Joyce Carol Oates's *First Love*—all by respected mainstream authors, all with vivid accounts of child abuse.

And once television got hold of the subject, how long could its seriousness last? On September 3, 1992, Oprah Winfrey had on her show a woman, Christina, and her stepfather, James, who had molested her when she was a child and whom Christina, in a television-friendly decision, was now confronting for the first time in sixteen years. This, Oprah tells Christina, is "an incredibly courageous thing for you to do. . . . And to—to do it on television in front of all of us, I think is—it's incredible." Oprah prolongs the suspense. "Are you ready?" she asks Christina, and Christina answers yes. "Are you prepared for it?" Oprah asks, and Christina again says yes. "James, could you come out?" says Oprah, and out comes the guilty James.

With prodding from Oprah, Christina asks him why he did what he did to her. James replies, "Tina, I'm more a victim of abuse also—wife abuse." Christina's mother, it turns out, emptied an automatic into James. (This was apparently before he started child-molesting.) She was, in Christina's words, "schizophrenic and a drunk" and used to push Christina and her sister into the bedroom with James. ("Her older sister was the one I did the most to," says James, in apparent self-defense.) There follows a desultory exchange, with Christina asking and James explaining. "There is such things as transference," he points out—he has been in psychotherapy—"and there is a lot of different reasons why everybody acts the way they do." Oprah meanwhile rains down pieties on them.

Finally, Christina forgives James, but by this time Oprah is through with them. "Coming up next," she says, "an entire family exposes their secret of incest for the first time. We will be right back." Then there's a commercial. In the face of this, it is hard to get one's brain around the fact that James actually spent nine years in the penitentiary for child-molesting. Child abuse has simply been added to the long list of problems—alcoholism, gambling, transvestism, the numberless "addictions"—on which television daily casts its glazed and earnest eye.

❧ ❧

But more than the entertainment industry, what shot a hole in the child protection movement was psychotherapy, with its insistence, as James put it, that "there is a lot of different reasons why everybody acts the way they do" and its belief that those reasons override criminal responsibility. Apart from discouraging confrontations and lawsuits, many therapists decided that the abusers were themselves abused, and therefore dissociative—indeed, multiples—and consequently not to blame. As a therapist said to an accused father interviewed by Pendergrast, "*You* didn't do anything, it was another part of you." This of course eliminates the moral issue. Michael

Yapko, in his *Suggestions of Abuse*, an otherwise valuable book on the recovered memory movement, addresses what he sees as the hard problem of how parents should respond when falsely accused by their children: "Admit to the abuse just to hold on to your child and you're forever branded as a monster. Deny it and you're forever branded a monster *and* a coward. The safest immediate solution is neither to confirm nor to deny the abuse, but to get someplace fast where these issues can be dealt with as openly and as fairly as possible"—in other words, a therapist's office. Is it possible that anyone on earth would knowingly make a false admission of child-molesting? If Yapko's daughter accused him falsely, would he really not say immediately, "I didn't do it"?[22]

Perhaps not, but if that is the case, then the outrage that was once attached to child abuse is gone. What remains is therapy, in which everyone can participate: abusers, abused, the whole family. Here, according to Roseanne Barr, is the course of therapy her family embarked on once she retrieved her memories: "We went every day and every night. Individual counseling for each of the kids, family therapy, my therapy, Tom's therapy, marriage counseling." Chances are, her therapist also went into therapy. According to the literature, counselors treating trauma victims often come down with posttraumatic stress disorder from listening to the patients' stories.[23]

The trauma is thus spread, and the crime diminished. Child abuse can now speak its name. *The Courage to Heal* recommends that you tell your children how you were molested. They suggest age-appropriate wording. To a six-year-old, for example, you might say, "When I was a little girl, my father made me touch his penis. That scared me a lot." ("Gee," the child is likely to think, "just like the scary dog next door.") In response to former Miss America Marilyn Van Derbur Atler's allegations that her father had sex with her for thirteen years, beginning when she was five, Atler's mother told *People* magazine, "I'll remember the good things he did. I can't let it ruin my life." And why should she? According to the theorists, he was probably molested too, though he can't go into therapy, because he's dead. Some of Mark Pendergrast's survivor intervie-wees actually sound bored with their abuse histories. "I'd be lying on the altar naked, with my legs spread," says one. "They'd lick blood and stuff off me."[24]

The corollary of this normalization is that child abuse may now become easier to commit. (Hacking thinks that the recovery liter-ature, like pornography, will give people ideas.) Marilyn Van Der-bur Atler has declared that her goal is "to make the word *incest* speakable and to take away the stigma we attach to it." She means the stigma attached to the victims, but the RM movement is also taking away the stigma attached to the crime.[25]

10

The Intellectuals

If the RM/MPD movement fit right in with the needs of the mass culture—with television, with the therapy industry—it also conformed to what was going on at the other end of the cultural ladder, in the universities, with the postmodern, poststructuralist, postcolonialist attack on the idea of knowledge. The belief in multiple identities, the rejection of science and of the ideal of objectivity, the redefinition of the past according to the standards of the present, the assertion that you have a right to construct your own truth and that anyone who asks you for proof of it is motivated by patriarchal prejudice: all are firmly supported by current academic thought.

The RM/MPD movement is also a product of the same politics that underlie postmodern thought. What we have seen in the United States since the seventies is a great contention of groups, each rightly claiming a history of oppression, each competing with the others for the society's attention, each probably also worrying that its own grievance will be cast into shadow by another's greater misfortune. Such worries become more serious as we move from the national to the international scene. In the last ten years, with the press reports from Bosnia, Chechnya, and the Middle East, not to speak of the African nations, we have probably been faced with the greatest-ever flood of information about violent harm being done to others. When thousands of people are dying in the forests of

Zaire, how do you get a hearing for the fact that you have a boring job and that your boyfriend beats you up?

A claim of childhood sexual abuse is one way. And if even this seems a little paltry compared to what is happening to others, *The Courage to Heal* suggests that you use for your own purposes the griefs of those others:

> If international issues like apartheid in South Africa eas-
> ily inflame you, let yourself get worked up over those
> problems, and then, when you're really angry, remind
> yourself that the mentality that allows whites to torture
> blacks is the same mentality that allowed your abuser to
> vent his twisted, uncontrolled needs, fear, and ruthless-
> ness on you. You can slide your own trauma in with the
> rest of the ills of the world, and you'll find yourself finally
> angry.[1]

In this competition for disadvantaged status, you have to pitch your claims as high as possible and then just dig in your heels.

Anyone who is confused by the debate over recovered memory and MPD should consider the controversy over Martin Bernal's 1991 *Black Athena*, a book of Afrocentric history in which it is claimed that ancient Greek culture was derived from Egyptian cul-ture and therefore that Western civilization is fundamentally African. When scholars asked Bernal for evidence—for example, archeological evidence that the Egyptians occupied Greece, as the book claimed—and, in the absence of evidence, challenged his account, Afrocentric historians interpreted this as an indication not of a weakness in Bernal's argument, but of its strength: the demand for evidence, they said, demonstrated the very prejudice that led to the cover-up of Europe's African roots. This is exactly the same logic used by the MPD authorities. If you question MPD or ask for proof of its theory, this just shows that you are in denial over child abuse and therefore part of the problem.

≫≫ ≪≪

In one recent development, "relational psychoanalysis," we can see the direct influence of postmodern thought on the recovered memory movement. Most RM/MPD therapy, as we saw, juggles two kinds of truth. Following the rules of "narrative truth," the patient puts together her story, but once that is done, she is allowed, even encouraged, to believe that she really was abused, and her case is added to the statistics on how child abuse causes MPD and other psychological disorders. What was narrative suddenly becomes historical. (Until the patient starts thinking about suing. Then, as noted, the therapist may gently remind her that her story is "narrative.")

The relational psychoanalysts, coming out of academic postmodernism, have tried to get rid of this double-talk by devising a therapy in which it is understood that the patient's truth is entirely "constructed"—in other words, narrative—and that the therapist collaborates in the construction. Patients and therapists together, says Helene Kafka of the William Alanson White Institute, "we embroider the story, employing twisted threads of memory, fantasy and experience, ours and theirs."[2] The analysts don't describe the resulting accounts as factually true.

You have to give these people credit. They are admitting—and consciously using—the factor that other RM treaters refuse to acknowledge: the therapist's influence over the patient's "memories." But one must ask how this works out in practice. As patient and therapist create the abuse story together, does the therapist keep reminding the patient that it is "constructed"? If so, this must be very frustrating to the patient. If not, the relational analysts may have some legal problems ahead—a possibility that they are apparently coming to realize. To quote relational analyst Adrienne Harris, of New York University, "No responsible clinician now sits at work without worrying that his or her listening . . . may be uncritical or coercive."[3] If Harris is worried about her "listening," what must Helene Kafka be thinking about her "embroidering"?

And what about the patients? How much are these unhappy women helped by constructing a maybe-true-maybe-false story with a postmodern-minded therapist? In a 1995 essay Joan Berzoff (Smith College) and Jaine Darwin (Harvard Medical School) tell the story of a patient, Laura, who was treated first by Berzoff for eleven years, then by Darwin for a further period. While Berzoff had diagnosed Laura with borderline personality disorder, Darwin espied MPD. She and Laura, Darwin writes, "were able to co-construct a history of all the traumas by documenting the birth of each alter." And the result? After what seems to have been about two years of therapy, Darwin and Laura "were not able to move beyond the beginning stages of this work." Laura dropped out of treatment; she couldn't afford it. She has since suffered "decline and further fragmentation."

Reviewing this depressing story, Berzoff expresses reservations about the MPD treatment, but she offers a consolation. Laura, she says, may be "aware that the diagnosis of MPD is also a social construction which represents a particular time in culture and in history. In the postmodern times in which we now live, the self is no longer conceptualized as unitary or continuous, but is seen as made up of multiple identities where each self contains 'a multitude of others, singing different melodies, different verses and with different rhythms, nor do these voices necessarily harmonize.'" That such thoughts are occurring to Laura, an unemployed industrial worker, seems doubtful. According to the article, she and her fifteen new personalities live on disability with two alcoholic roommates. She too is probably alcoholic; she was drinking heavily during her MPD therapy, though Darwin says that was "done by a 16-year-old alter." Laura told her therapists that she had suffered years of sexual assaults by her father and brother, but there is no mention of anyone's suggesting a legal remedy, nor would the courts be interested in "co-constructed" memories.[4]

Women

What of the patients' responsibility for the MPD epidemic? In any single case, the appearance of MPD may be explainable by the factors named before: the patient is highly hypnotizable, has dissociative symptoms, and is in bad trouble; the therapist believes in MPD; drugs are prescribed; there is insurance. But to account for a whole social phenomenon, in which thousands of women, in a short space of time, decide that they are housing an average of sixteen personalities in addition to their main one, we have to look for an additional factor. The answer, I believe, is the women's movement.

While feminism rescued many women from positions of dependency, it left others behind, notably a large number of working-class women. (I do not speak of the poor, because, not having the money for psychotherapy, they tend not to be diagnosed with MPD.) Many of these women had the same grim lives as their mothers: early pregnancy, unkind husbands or boyfriends, boring jobs, little money, no education. But in the post-sixties period, they were also deprived of the protections their mothers had: a strong family structure and, with the rise of feminism, the belief that their fate was woman's fate. As a Marxist would say, they were deprived of false consciousness. All around them, and especially on television, they saw women who did not share this "woman's fate." Whence the discrepancy? How had they missed the boat?

So new troubles—bitterness, a sense of failure—were added to their load. This process helps to explain the great outbreak of female disorders in the last few decades: the eating disorders, "codependency," and so on. In her book *I'm Dysfunctional, You're Dysfunctional*, Wendy Kaminer tells of women in recovery groups getting up and accusing themselves of being passive, submissive. "It is as if they were discovering what is wrong with femininity for the first time," Kaminer writes. "These are women whom feminism bypassed."[1]

So are the multiples, with the difference that their disorder in a way supplies what they lacked. Suddenly, with the MPD diagnosis and the establishment of the abuse history, they are no longer weak, downtrodden. They are courageous—veterans, "survivors." Furthermore, they are unusually intelligent, an article of faith in the MPD literature. (Sybil is said by Schreiber to have had an IQ of 170.)[2] Most important of all, they are creative, as evidenced by their elaborate disorder. In a way, they are artists. Sybil was a painter, and one of her alters was an accomplished pianist.

Lured by the hope that she too may have unmined creativity, the budding multiple is soon given a chance to exercise it, by fashioning the alters that her therapist is asking to meet. As she does so, she becomes many good things that she was not before. She has male alters, with strength and independence; child alters, innocent and sweet; devil alters, with the power to do harm; hussy alters, with sexual courage; patrician alters, with clipped speech and a taste for opera. (In *The Discovery of the Unconscious*, Ellenberger reports that nineteenth-century servant girls, when hypnotized, often developed upper-class accents.) If she embarks on SRA, she may rise yet higher on the social scale. Patricia Burgus, under Bennett Braun's care, traced her family's history back to the Middle Ages, when her forbears were "supreme monarchs of the royal blood." From what she told Ofshe and Watters, she also remembered having been Catherine the Great in a former life.[3]

In addition to these new qualities, the woman now has a job to do. She whose thoughts, let alone her writings, have rarely been asked for before must now keep a journal, which her therapist will read. She has to map her "system," a project that according to one expert may take as long as a year.[4] (Jenny Walters Harris, of *Suffer the Child,* had an alter who developed her own, independent MPD, with a full constellation of alters. Such complications require a redrawing of the map.) In the treatment hour she has to take part in "inner group therapy" and "inner board room" sessions.

Above all, she has to tell stories: the story of her abuse, the story of the lives of her alters, in collaboration with her therapist. Colin Ross describes working with a patient to rescue a child alter who is imprisoned in a porn factory. He hypnotizes the patient. Then they create a story together:

> I [Ross] went into the building, opened the door, and called the alter over. She was in a room in which pornographic movies were being made. She and other children, many drugged or drunk, were taking part in hard-core sex while being filmed. I was able to accompany the child out of the room because nobody but her could see or hear me. In the hall, there was a struggle as she tried to get away, and we were able to escape from the building.

With other patients, Ross says, "the therapist will stay in the present while an alter reports back on its mission to rescue other alters, destroy castle walls, disarm internal computers, rebuild architecture, create safe places, or carry out other missions." In other words, patient and therapist, drawing on their fantasy lives, script an action movie together. It is also, of course, a sex movie. In another account of the porn factory rescue, Ross says that the child alter "described in detail the sodomy, fellatio, cunnilingus and other acts the children were forced to perform."[5]

Other multiples create weepers. Here is Jane Phillips, in her MPD memoir *The Magic Daughter*, describing the "integration" of her child alters, "The Kids." The Kids are keeping up a brave front about their imminent extinction. Then they remember their stuffed toy Badger:

> The Kids broke down. "Who will take care of Badger? He doesn't like to be all by himself."
>
> "Poor Badger," [the therapist] said. "What do you think we should do?"
>
> The Kids leaned toward him and said with a certain fierceness, "Make The Grown-ups promise they will always take care of Badger. You make them *promise,*" they insisted. "Cause we're worried about Badger."
>
> "I will," he said gently.

This is actually being enacted in the office, with the therapist as the therapist and Phillips as The Kids. Eugene Bliss, the man who installed the alter "Dr. Bliss" in one of his patients, said that working with multiples was "live theater"; it made him feel "like an ancient thaumaturge." If it excites the therapist, how much more fascinating must it be to the patient? If she wasn't creative before, she is now.[6]

The new multiple enjoys many other benefits. There are the accessories: the board games, the pen pals. There are MPD newsletters, eager to publish her poems. There are clubs she can join. (According to Hacking, the Multiple Personality Consortium of Asheville, North Carolina, has regular get-togethers: trips to theme parks, finger-painting nights for child alters.) She gets special consideration from her family. One Christmas, Vynette Hamanne's husband, advised by Dr. Humenansky that he must accept his wife's fifty-odd alters, bought a different present for each of them—crayons for the child alters, lingerie for the sexpots, and so on. The patient also has the pleasure of knowing that she has an interesting illness, one that is the subject of movies and books. Indeed, she herself might be described in a book—this is what Humenansky promised Carlson—or at least get to go on TV.[7]

But the crucial pay-off was the chance to be creative. MPD therapy gave patients the thing that they could not get from the society, an interesting job. Chris Sizemore (Eve) has said that being a multiple was "fun" and that when she recovered, the "magic" went out of her life.[8] Learning from her experience, other multiples have declined to integrate. Truddi Chase, author of the MPD memoir *When Rabbit Howls*, still has her ninety-two personalities. They are called "the Troops," and that is who is listed as the author on the book's title page: "The Troops, for Truddi Chase." Actually, for most patients, life as a multiple cannot be fun; these women have too many problems. But the problems may be far more bearable when called this fancy name, multiple personality disorder, and combined with this exciting therapy.

Of course, to become a full-fledged multiple, the woman has to claim that she was sexually assaulted as a child. How likely is it, the MPD believers ask, that someone would make up such an appalling story? Rather likely, given the inducements just described—plus the one-third-of-women statistic, to make it seem normal; plus drugs, to confuse her; plus hypnosis, to get her over the hump. Furthermore, many women don't have to make up the story. They *were* abused, and as Elizabeth Carlson discovered, to expand on that is not hard. Also, a substantial percentage of multiples—nearly half of them, according to one survey—report having been sexually assaulted as adults, so that they have no difficulty imagining themselves as victims of violent men. And if they have any political awareness, they may not need an actual assault. In the words of social psychologist Carol Tavris, "The sexual abuse explanation, if not literal, is a brilliant figurative metaphor for the abuse that many women do feel they have suffered in society—for their powerlessness, for their vulnerability."[9]

Indeed, political sentiments are not required. In its report on Ann Norris, the twenty-seven-alter patient who was claiming that she had spiders stuffed up her vagina by her mother, the *Frontline* documentary "Divided Memories" included an interview with the mother, who filled in some family history. When Ann was two, her parents separated, and the mother, in her sorrow, withdrew from Ann and Ann's older brother. The only child for whom she could express love was her new baby—a situation that continued after she and her husband reconciled a year and a half later. She would look into Ann's eyes, she recalls, and they said to her, "'What's wrong, Mom? . . . Why aren't you giving something to me?' And I couldn't." In other words, Ann, at age two, abruptly lost both her mother's love and her father. How does a person remember such a catastrophe, one that occurred, furthermore, before the period normally available to adult recall? Spiders up the vagina seem a fairly good metaphor. In looking for the cause of suffering, we are always hoping that it won't be the same old thing: no love, no kindness, no money. It will be something else, we think—spiders, MPD.

≫ ≪

Many women, then, had reason to take shelter in multiple personality disorder. It restored their dignity; it gave them a career. And if it wasn't real, neither, in that sense, are most of the mental disorders listed in *DSM*. They are simply organizing concepts that people of a certain time and place have come up with to explain unhappiness. In a time of extreme female unhappiness, why not organize that problem as MPD? The question about MPD should not be whether the diagnosis is real but whether it is helpful.

It is not. As noted, there is no decent scientific evidence demonstrating that MPD therapy cures people, nor is it likely to, since, by breaking the personality up into parts—parts the "host" can then disavow—it does exactly the opposite of what good therapy is supposed to do: make the patient take responsibility for the person she truly is.

But forget the patient for a moment. MPD is a disorder that involves the gravest possible social problems: the oppression of women, the mistreatment of children, poverty. And by translating those problems into purely personal matters, it has defused them as topics of public concern. Apart from their favorite topic, child-molesting, the MPD writers barely mention social issues. The physical abuse of children is far more common than sexual abuse. Janice Haaken asks the hard question: "Is fondling a child worse than beating her with a belt? Is an episode of touching a child's genitals, or having a child touch an adult's genitals, more traumatic than chronic neglect or emotional abandonment?"[10] Some people would say yes—the MPD writers evidently would—but as we saw earlier, emotional neglect in childhood seems more likely than sexual abuse to lead to adult mental disorders. And physical neglect is responsible for the majority of child mistreatment fatalities.

As for poverty, study after study has shown its correlation with child abuse. According to a 1996 report by the U.S. Department of Health and Human Services, a child in a family earning less than $15,000 per year is twelve to sixteen times more likely to be physically abused, and eighteen times more likely to be sexually abused, than a child in a family earning over $30,000 per year. These statistics must be viewed critically, because the poor are far more prone to come into contact with social agencies that would discover and report abuse. But even if we cut the numbers in half, the children of the poor are still six to nine times more likely to suffer abuse. This fact is a great embarrassment, both to conservatives opposing anti-poverty programs and to liberals fearful of stigmatizing the poor. It is also something that the RM/MPD writers clearly prefer to forget, for poverty is almost never addressed in their writings. Repeatedly we are told that most multiples are middle class, and repeatedly, in the case histories, we find that they come from hard-pressed families. Margo Rivera reports that in a government-funded Canadian survey of 185 multiples, more than half had been on some form of public assistance, and one out of five had been on welfare as children.[11]

Money, of course, affects not only a girl's chance of being abused but her chance of getting over it. Dara Culhane, a medical anthropologist interviewed in Carol Tavris's *The Mismeasure of Woman*, says that according to her information middle-class survivors of childhood sexual abuse generally recover well—actually, she says, they often "overachieve"—whereas their poorer counterparts tend to drift into alcohol and drug abuse. So why, Culhane asks, is the problem said to be sexual abuse rather than poverty? Culhane goes on, "It's as though the poor woman [with a sex abuse history] is sitting there and saying, 'Shall I go and get my Master's Degree or shall I go to the local bar? Oh, I guess I'll go to the bar.' And the middle-class woman has the same set of choices: 'Shall I go to the bar, or shall I go and get my law degree? I'll flip a coin; oh, it tells me to get a law degree.'"[12]

It is probably no coincidence that the child protection movement, with its focus on evil individuals rather than social causes, peaked in a period of rising conservatism in American politics. In the 1980s the federal government cut program after program aimed at helping the children of the poor. As anthropologists Nancy Scheper-Hughes and Howard Stein have written, "*The time of greatest public outcry against child abuse is also the time of widespread, official planning of sacrifice of children in public policy.*"[13] (Italics theirs.) The one made the other possible.

≫ ≪

What the RM/MPD movement has done to the cause of children it has also done to the cause of women. Multiple personality disorder is a form of hysteria, and like other forms of hysteria, stretching back many centuries, it is a metaphor for female powerlessness. The same goes for abuse claims; even when they are genuine, they are metaphors. Take away the thing they represent, the sense—in life, not just in bed—of being weak, being used, and the woman would get over the abuse, as most women do.

In centuries past, hysteria was dealt with by medicalizing it. The woman had an "illness," the doctor was called, and that was the end of the political issue. In our own time, with the women's movement, one might have expected things to go differently. And they have gone the same. The doctor was called, the MPD doctor this time, and the political problem was once again called an individual problem, psychiatric this time. A number of writers have pointed out the resemblance between MPD and what anthropologist I. M. Lewis called "peripheral possession" in traditional societies.[14] This is a form of spirit possession that afflicts people low on the social ladder, notably women. For example, a woman married to a neglectful man may become inhabited by a spirit who demands that he stage an expensive ceremony, requiring that she have new clothes; in polygamous societies, a woman who has had a miscarriage may produce a spirit forbidding her husband to take a second wife. In such cases, the man must obey: the spirit has spoken. But the laws of the society need not be changed. Small concessions are made so that large injustices may remain.

MPD therapy is the same. The woman is given relief, but at the same time she is designated as sick—therefore marginal—and efforts are made to prevent her from coming into contact with social institutions, such as the lawcourts, that would take her complaint as a matter of public concern. All this reminds one very distinctly of Thomas Szasz's argument, made in the sixties, but now (because of the rise of biomedical psychiatry) widely forgotten, that the function of psychiatry is to defuse political problems by converting them into spurious medical problems.

Some feminist writers have complained about the politics of the RM/MPD movement. I will name the ones I have read—Louise Armstrong, Janice Haaken, Wendy Kaminer, Ruth Leys, Debbie Nathan, Elaine Showalter, Carol Tavris—in order to show how few they are. In general, this trend, so damaging to the interests of women, has been enthusiastically supported by feminists. In the case of the recovered-memory movement, it was started by feminists, and belongs to them.

That is not true of MPD. While the diagnosis has been endorsed by feminists and though many of the therapists treating MPD are women, the top of the field belongs to men. With one exception,

Cornelia Wilbur, who died in 1992, all the most important MPD theorists have been male. Why is that? Perhaps because, though garlanded with feminist ideas—above all, the sex abuse claim—MPD is so profoundly antifeminist that the female theorists instinctively backed off from it.

MPD, it seems likely, was born of psychiatry's aversion to a certain kind of female patient. Recall that women who are diagnosed as multiples have been in the mental health system for an average of seven years, with little or no improvement. (Colin Ross writes that many of his patients are "dumps," cases referred to him by other therapists who don't care what he calls them—MPD, whatever—as long as he takes over.[15]) Not only are these patients unresponsive to treatment, they are immensely difficult.

Many writers agree that a large proportion of multiples, if they were not called multiples, would be given the diagnosis of borderline personality disorder (as, for example, were Colin Ross's "Pam" and Berzoff and Davis's "Laura" before they were rediagnosed as MPs). Borderline, writes psychiatrist Irvin Yalom, is "the word that strikes terror in the heart of the middle-aged comfort-seeking psychiatrist."[16] Borderlines are in a constant state of emotional crisis: attention-seeking, insecure, impulsive, self-destructive. One minute they are hanging on you; the next minute, they are cursing you. Many report childhood abuse. Many have episodes of dissociation or paranoia. The great majority—about 75 percent, says *DSM*—are women. Borderline personality disorder, then, is a portrait of femininity out of control. (This diagnosis, together with MPD, came in with feminism. Like MPD, it was first listed in *DSM* in 1980.) How to get these women back in control? One way is by repairing their femininity, getting them to conform again to the time-honored pattern of womanhood.

That is what MPD is, point for point: an image of woman as she once was, or was said to be. In the alternating personalities we have woman's notorious volatility—"La donna è mobile." In the contest between the child alters and the hussy alters, we have the madonna-

and-whore split. With the amnesia and the uncontrolled switching, we have woman's long-recognized moral incapacity, the fact that she cannot be held responsible for her behavior. (Freud: "Women have but little sense of justice.") In the hidden cause, the childhood sexual trauma, we get further essential components of femininity. Women are childlike, passive, wounded. Above all, they are sex; they are what's between their legs. In the abreactions, meanwhile, we see woman's well-known tendency to have hysterics, fits, weeping spells, while men stand by patiently, waiting for the storm to pass. And in the rest of the therapy, with its relentless focus on the woman's feelings—with the journal-writing, the history-exploring, the alter debriefing—we have woman's famous subjectivity, her preference for emotion over action, her status as a creature of phone calls and girl talks. More than a disorder, MPD is a memory: a memory of women, invoked by men.

I have listed a number of characteristics here, but they can be boiled down to two, sex and childlikeness. In MPD therapy, the woman is visualized as a nymphet. If one were brutal, one might suggest that this is an erotic fantasy on the part of the MPD theorists. Men have always preferred their sex partners young. (On the cover of *Michelle Remembers* is a little blue-eyed girl, hugging her doll. And smack in the middle is a shot of the child's little crotch. The artist is looking up the dress of a five-year-old.) But one does not have to be brutal to consider how satisfying this image might be to the patient, even one who, in another part of her mind, is revolted by the idea of child-molesting. For a very long time, the most advantageous thing a woman could be in our society was childlike and sexual at the same time. After Marilyn Van Derbur Atler retrieved her abuse memories, Pendergrast interviewed her sister, Gwen Mitchell, who said that she too had been molested by this father, and had never forgotten. "I thought I was the only one," Mitchell told Pendergrast. "Mother used to say that he liked me the best. He called me the Countess, so I believed I was special and the only one."[17]

With the sex-child status comes blamelessness. The woman is not responsible for the sex. Indeed, she is not responsible for anything. That is the whole point of the alters. They are *alter*—Latin for "other." To quote psychiatrist Seymour Halleck, "To the extent that we accept the separateness or autonomy of differing personalities [in MPD], we cease to describe a morally or legally recognizable person. We are . . . dealing with a collection of partial persons who have no collective capacity for responsibility." (Or, in the words of Robert Louis Stevenson, "It was Hyde, after all, and Hyde alone, that was guilty. Jekyll . . . awoke again to his good qualities seemingly unimpaired.")[18] Blamelessness is the central underlying theme of the MPD literature. Even writers who don't believe in the disorder don't hold the woman responsible. The False Memory Syndrome Foundation blames the therapists, not the patients. But of course the ability to be blamed is the basis of adulthood in the moral sense.

As I said, the main attraction of MPD for the patient is probably that she is given an interesting project, that she is at last taken seriously. And the tragedy of the disorder is that the opposite is true: she is not taken seriously. Who are we kidding here? The doll collection of alters, the adventures in the porn factory: this is a disorder that could have been made up by a child. And what of the internal contradictions? According to the Putnam group's 1986 survey, 87 percent of multiples show frequent and spontaneous switching; 85 percent have child alters; 70 percent have violent alters. So these women are uncontrollably metamorphosing into violent or infantile personalities. Why, then, are they permitted to drive cars? Why do we allow children to remain in their care? And if, as the Putnam group's survey found, 98 percent are amnesic, how does one explain that they remember to come to their therapy appointments? There seems to be only one answer: the therapists don't actually believe the patients. MPD is a game, and a bargain. The patient forfeits the privileges of being an adult—self-knowledge, moral agency.

In return, she is given back the sex-child dream, the cotton panties of yesteryear.

What would happen if the patient *were* taken seriously? In the literature there are a few accounts of the therapist being offered an alter and refusing. Irvin Yalom, in his psychotherapy casebook *Love's Executioner*, describes his treatment of a patient he calls Marge, age thirty-five. Marge is panicked; she is depressed. "Everything else about her—multiple suicide attempts, eating disorder, early sexual abuse by her father, episodic psychotic thinking, twenty-three years of psychotherapy—shouted 'borderline.'" By day, Marge sits in Yalom's office and berates herself. By night, she calls him at home to berate herself. Then, one day in therapy something strange happens:

> In the middle of her dirge, she suddenly closed her eyes—not in itself unusual since she often went into an autohypnotic state during the session. I had long before decided not to take the bait—not to follow her into the hypnoidal state—but instead would call her out of it. I said, "Marge," and was about to utter the rest of the sentence, "Will you please come back?" when I heard a strange and powerful voice come out of her mouth: "You don't know me." . . .
>
> "Who are you?" I asked.
>
> "Me! Me!" And then the transformed Marge jumped up and proceeded to prance around the office, peering into bookcases, straightening pictures, and inspecting my furniture. It was Marge, but it was not Marge. Everything but the clothing had changed—her carriage, her face, her self-assurance, her walk.[19]

This apparition is very like Eve Black in *The Three Faces of Eve*, and it was probably based on her. (Yalom does not say this, but he seems to know it, for he gives Marge the same last name as Eve's host personality: White.) She is as vivacious and bold as Marge is whiny and self-demeaning. She does mocking imitations of Marge; she flirts with Yalom. And he responds. Like Thigpen and Cleckley with Eve Black, he falls half in love with her. But unlike Thigpen and Cleckley with Eve Black, he decides to have nothing to do with her. The title of this chapter in Yalom's book is "Therapeutic Monogamy." "I had promised myself to Marge," he writes. "If I consorted with 'Me,' it would be catastrophic for Marge; she'd become a bit player." So he remains faithful. Every time Marge starts to go into trance, threatening to release "Me," he says, "Marge, come back!"[20]

Meanwhile, though, he uses "Me," by "feeding" her to Marge: "The feeding technique was to repeat one standard question, 'Marge, what would "she" say if she were here?'" Eventually, it began to work:

> One day when I saw her timidly scanning the objects in my office, I said, "Go ahead, speak, Marge. Speak for 'her.'"
>
> Marge took a deep breath and revved up her voice. "If you're going to pretend to be a Jewish intellectual, why not furnish your office like one?"[21]

Marge's therapy had to be terminated after a year and a half because Yalom was leaving on sabbatical. Even then, however, she was substantially improved. She panicked only rarely; she had made two friends, taken up a hobby—photography. "She looked better, dressed better; she sat up straight; she wore patterned stockings."[22] Clinging before, she now treated Yalom as an equal. A little shyly, she too, like "her," began flirting with Yalom. After a few months, they had stopped talking about "her." As Yalom says, they had sucked all the juice out of her.

More heartening, however, than what Marge achieved in this therapy is what Yalom achieved. Offered the old arrangement—a respectable, downtrodden, sex-and-aggression-disavowing wife and a brassy woman on the side—he turned it down. Instead of allowing Marge to disassociate herself from "her," he forced Marge to keep this part of herself inside, where it belonged—a beacon of remembered hope.

※ ※

The late nineteenth-century outbreak of hysteria occurred under a specific set of conditions: widespread, bitter intellectual debate, a war between biological and psychological psychiatry, a fascination with the occult, an obsession with sex and an explosion of pornography, a new concern over cruelty to children, feminism and opposition to feminism. From about 1920 to 1970 hysteria died down, and what cases there were got distributed among various "neurotic" diagnoses. Then, in the late twentieth century, the conditions that had produced nineteenth-century hysteria came to the fore again, and so did hysteria. It looked a little different this time. Somatizing, the expression of psychological distress as physical complaints, tends to vary in direct relation to the psychological naïveté of the patient. The more ignorant the patient is about psychology, the more he or (usually) she will somatize. Nineteenth-century hysterics developed somatic symptoms: paralyses, convulsions, blindness. Twentieth-century hysterics, more psychologically sophisticated, developed psychological symptoms, notably multiple personality disorder. But it was the same condition and it was handled in the same way—as a medical, not a political, problem. Will we do this every hundred years?

Academic feminists, especially in literary criticism, have a kind of cult of nineteenth-century hysteria. They regard it as the necessarily strangulated language of women trying to express themselves in a patriarchal culture. Like so much else in contemporary academic thought, this idea seems to have come from France. As Elaine Showalter relates, the participants at a 1972 feminist conference in

Paris chanted, "Nous sommes toutes des hystériques!" ("We are all hysterics!") The widely revered psychoanalytic theorist Jacques Lacan said that he wanted to "hystericize" psychoanalysis, make it playful and mysterious again. His followers, the French feminists, called for a new hysteria, "a woman's language of the body, or pre-oedipal semiotics," as Showalter describes it.[23] These people should be told that in the United States we have had a new hysteria, and that its victims are going to need many more years before they recover from its pre-oedipal semiotics.

If one were conspiratorially minded, one might suggest that MPD was an antifeminist campaign. (In the 1970s, the decade in which the disorder was reborn, more women entered the paid work-force than at any other time in history without benefit of a major war.) But it was not a conspiracy, it was a reflex of our current politics. The pattern goes like this. A historically disadvantaged group knocks on the door of the society, protesting its position. The society feels guilty, and offers reparation. Some mechanisms of reparation—affirmative action, for example—are practical and useful, aimed at giving the group an actual place in the world, but they take effect slowly. In the interim, various comforts are offered, for example, the idea that the society works not by one set of truths but by many, and that every group is entitled to its own "narrative." Fed this fantasy, the disadvantaged group goes off and makes up its narrative, until, very soon, the story becomes too extravagant. It claims that Greek culture was African or that one-third of American women were molested as girls; it contradicts the society's most cherished beliefs. At that point it is attacked, and then the situation becomes clear: that in this promise of an alternative truth, what the disadvantaged were given was not a place in the world but a sort of refugee camp, where they went on dreaming the same dreams as before, based on their history of powerlessness. Women are still in the refugee camp, and multiple personality disorder was one of the dreams.

⁂

Shortly after her lawsuit was concluded, Elizabeth Carlson was diagnosed with lupus. Taking her two children (her marriage had now ended), she moved to Florida. There she was also diagnosed with fibromyalgia, a degenerative muscle disorder. In 1997 she had a small stroke. Today, when she goes out, she has to use a walker. She is forty-five. I asked her whether she blames herself for her MPD-therapy disaster. "No," she replied. "Or not any more. It could have happened to anyone, given the right conditions." In 1993, she founded the National Association Against Fraud in Psychotherapy, and despite her health problems, she still works, counseling retrac-

Chapter 1: One Woman's Story

1. This figure is cited by many authorities—for example, Colin A. Ross, *Multiple Personality Disorder*, p. 68.

2. Ellen Bass and Laura Davis, *The Courage to Heal*, 1st ed., pp. 20 (one third of women abused), 43 (explanation of MPD); 3rd ed., p. 430 ("I remember splitting").

3. Frank W. Putnam, *Diagnosis and Treatment of Multiple Personality Disorder*, p. 174.

4. Forty thousand new cases: Colin A. Ross, *Dissociative Identity Disorder*, p. 227. (This estimate is probably high.) Mean of sixteen alters per patient: Colin A. Ross and others, "Multiple Personality Disorder: An Analysis of 236 Cases," p. 246.

5. Patient with forty-five hundred personalities: Richard P. Kluft, "The Phenomenology and Treatment of Extremely Complex Multiple Personality Disorder," p. 52. Wisconsin case: reported in Doug Erickson, "Cool Recalls Ritual to Rid Her of Evil," p. A1. "Sages, lobsters": George K. Ganaway, "Historical Versus Narrative Truth," p. 209.

6. "I didn't feel anything": Mark Pendergrast, *Victims of Memory*, p. 348. "Every time you cut": Ross speaking on CBC Television, *Fifth Estate*, "Mistaken Identities," 9 Nov. 1993. "Yet it's been a time": Letter from "Carla," *Cutting Edge*, Winter 1996, p. 8.

7. Carol S. North and others, *Multiple Personalities, Multiple Disorders*, p. 13.

8. "Cry out": Colin A. Ross, *Multiple Personality Disorder*, p. 249. Stroke during abreaction: David Calof, presentation at Advances in Treating Survivors of Sexual Abuse conference, Feb. 1993, quoted in *False Memory Syndrome Foundation Newsletter*, Jan. 1996, p. 6. Braun and nine-hour abreactions: Bennett G. Braun, presentation to 1992 Midwestern Conference on Child Sexual Abuse and Incest, summarized in Richard Ofshe and Ethan Watters, *Making Monsters*, p. 246.

9. George Ganaway, interview with author.

10. "I have found": Ross, *Multiple Personality Disorder*, p. 282. "If you take enough drugs": quoted in Eric L. Nelson and Paul Simpson, "First Glimpse," p. 127.

11. "Recollections obtained during hypnosis": American Medical Association, Council on Scientific Affairs, "Scientific Status of Refreshing Recollection by the Use of Hypnosis," p. 1918. "When a physician": quoted in Corbett H. Thigpen and Hervey M. Cleckley, *The Three Faces of Eve* (rev. ed.), p. 162. Former lives as chimpanzees: M. V. Kline, "A Note on 'Primate-Like' Behavior Induced Through Hypnosis."

12. 1983 experiment: Jean-Roch Laurence and Campbell Perry, "Hypnotically Created Memory Among Highly Hypnotizable Subjects," summarized in Ofshe and Watters, *Making Monsters*, pp. 144–145. Yapko findings: Michael D. Yapko, *Suggestions of Abuse*, pp. 57–58.

13. Ross, *Multiple Personality Disorder*, p. 274.

14. "This could be someone," "MPD: The Syndrome of the '90s": cited in Jeanne Albronda Heaton and Nona Leigh Wilson, *Tuning in Trouble*, p. 134.

15. Flora Rheta Schreiber, *Sybil*, p. 110.

16. Ross, *Multiple Personality Disorder*, p. 48.

17. "Travesty," "On the basis": quoted in Pam Belluck, "'Memory' Therapy Leads to a Lawsuit and Big Settlement," p. A13.

18. Paul R. McHugh, "Foreword," in August Piper Jr., *Hoax and Reality*, p. x.

Chapter 2: The History

1. Henri F. Ellenberger, *The Discovery of the Unconscious*, p. 112. In addition to Ellenberger, a good source on how psychiatric symptoms change over time is Edward Shorter, *From Paralysis to Fatigue*.

2. Findings on comorbidity in MPD patients are summarized by North and others, *Multiple Personalities, Multiple Disorders*, pp. 48–49. Colin A. Ross, in his *Satanic Ritual Abuse*, p. 78, states that in his experience the average MPD patient meets the diagnostic criteria for eleven different psychiatric disorders.

3. See, for example, North and others, *Multiple Personalities, Multiple Disorders*, p. 183: "Current knowledge does not at this time sufficiently justify the validity of MPD as a separate diagnosis." Another discussion of the validity of the diagnosis can be found in Piper's *Hoax and Reality*, Chapter 2. In a 1999 survey of psychiatrists by Harrison Pope Jr. and his colleagues ("Attitudes Toward DSM-IV Dissociative Disorder Diagnoses Among Board-Certified American Psychiatrists"), only about one-fifth believed that there was strong evidence for the validity of MPD, and only about one-third felt that it should be included without reservations in *DSM*.

4. Colin A. Ross, *The Osiris Complex*, p. 60.

5. "Misteria": The term is Dr. Silas Weir Mitchell's, quoted in Roy Porter, "The Body and the Mind, the Doctor and the Patient," p. 245. Briquet's male-female ratio: cited in Ellenberger, *The Discovery of the Unconscious*, p. 122. Ellenberger's book was my primary source for the history of hysteria and MPD. I have also used Ian Hacking, *Rewriting the Soul*; Mark S. Micale, *Approaching Hysteria*; Michael G. Kenny, *The Passion of Ansel Bourne*; W. S. Taylor and Mabel F. Martin, "Multiple Personality"; and Sander L. Gilman and others, *Hysteria Beyond Freud*, with essays by Helen King, G. S. Rousseau, Roy Porter, Elaine Showalter, and Gilman.

6. G. S. Rousseau, "'A Strange Pathology,'" p. 98.

7. Jean-Baptiste Louyer-Villermay, quoted in Elaine Showalter, *Hystories*, p. 64.

8. Vibrator and hysteria: These are the findings of Rachel P. Maines, *The Technology of Orgasm* (1999), summarized in Natalie Angier, "In the History of Gynecology, a Surprising Chapter," p. F5. Apparently, the treatment worked, though, interestingly, it required repeated applications.

9. Micale, *Approaching Hysteria*, p. 190.

10. Quoted in Elaine Showalter, "Hysteria, Feminism, and Gender," p. 287.

11. Lisa Tickner, *The Spectacle of Women*; Showalter, "Hysteria, Feminism, and Gender."

12. Described in Taylor and Martin, "Multiple Personality," p. 289.

13. Georges Guillain, cited in Ellenberger, *The Discovery of the Unconscious*, p. 101.

14. In his 1984 book *The Assault on Truth*, Jeffrey Masson argued that a major factor in Freud's abandonment of the seduction theory was lack of courage in the face of colleagues scandalized by his claims of widespread sexual perversity. Mikkel Borch-Jacobsen, in his 1996 essay "Neurotica," points out that many writers prior to Freud, notably the sexologists of the 1880s, had already explored the subject of perversity. Borch-Jacobsen's view is that Freud's main reason for laying aside the seduction theory was his worry—and his colleagues' accusations—that his patients' abuse memories were the product of suggestion on his part. Borch-Jacobsen goes on to argue that the theory of the Oedipus complex was a way for Freud to get out of the seduction hypothesis without revealing his role in creating the abuse memories. He had not made a mistake; he had not implanted the memories. The patients had made the mistake, by locating the source of those memories in reality rather than fantasy. According to Borch-Jacobsen, all of Freudian theory is an extension of this cover-up: "The Oedipus complex, infantile sexuality, the wish-fantasies, all of Freud's self-proclaimed 'discoveries' are arbitrary constructions designed to explain away his patients' stories of

incest and perversion while simultaneously excusing the method that had provoked them. . . . Masson, feminists, and child-abuse activists tell us that Freud covered up the despicable actions of pedophile fathers. Not so. He covered up the hypnosis that allowed him to obtain the stories, while leaving the astonished world with an Oedipal unconscious. . . . True, we are all obsessed with incest, but do we know that it is because we are living in a world fashioned by the hypnotic pact between Dr. Freud and his patients?" (p. 43)

15. Jones quoted in B. Hart, "The Conception of Dissociation," cited in Nicholas P. Spanos, *Multiple Identities and False Memories*, p. 225.

16. Ross, *Multiple Personality Disorder*, p. 181.

Chapter 5: The Epidemic

1. Statements by Rush: quoted in Louise Armstrong, *Kiss Daddy Goodnight*, p. 133.

2. Bass and Davis, *The Courage to Heal*, 1st ed., p. 21.

3. All these books were sources for my discussion of the recovered memory movement.

4. Bass and Davis, *The Courage to Heal*, 1st ed., p. 35. In the third edition of *The Courage to Heal*, presumably in response to criticisms of such checklists, Bass and Davis insert the statement, "The lists are not a diagnostic tool and are not intended to serve as a way to determine whether or not you've been sexually abused" (p. 38). Then they go right ahead and say, "Look at the following lists and ask yourself how you've been affected" (p. 38).

5. In the widely publicized Ramona case, tried in California in 1994, part of the evidence offered to show that Gary Ramona had molested his daughter Holly was that she did not like mayonnaise, cream soups, or melted cheese. In 1989 Holly Ramona entered therapy for bulimia. At the initial visit the therapist reportedly told Holly and her mother that 70 to 80 percent of bulimics were survivors of childhood sexual abuse. Holly denied having been abused, but after several months of therapy, she began having "flashbacks" of molestation by her father. Eventually she accused him of having

raped her. Gary Ramona's wife divorced him, and he lost his job. In 1994 he brought a malpractice suit against Holly's therapist and the hospital where she was treated. He was awarded approximately half a million dollars.

6. Cited in False Memory Syndrome Foundation, "Frequently Asked Questions," p. 12.

7. "Many women don't have memories": Bass and Davis, *The Courage to Heal*, 1st ed., p. 81. "The existence of profound disbelief": Renee Fredrickson, *Repressed Memories*, p. 171. "If you think you were abused": *The Courage to Heal*, 1st ed., p. 22. This last sentence became so notorious that in the third edition (see p. 23) the authors modified it to read, "If you genuinely think you were abused and your life shows the symptoms, there's a strong likelihood that you were."

8. Poole survey: Debra A. Poole and others, "Psychotherapy and the Recovery of Memories of Childhood Sexual Abuse," p. 430. "You know, in my experience": Susan Forward and C. Buck, *Betrayal of Innocence*, quoted in Elizabeth Loftus and Katherine Ketcham, *The Myth of Repressed Memory*, p. 151.

9. "Write about whatever": Laura Davis, *The Courage to Heal Workbook*, p. 217. "I lie there": Betsy Petersen, *Dancing with Daddy*, p. 70.

10. "Saying to yourself": Fredrickson, *Repressed Memories*, p. 32. "Validate" your "reality": Bass and Davis, *The Courage to Heal*, 3rd ed., p. 336.

11. Bass and Davis, *The Courage to Heal*, 3rd ed., p. 332. This rule is an adaptation of the slogan "Believe the child" that accompanied the day-care scandals of the 1980s. In fact, the investigators involved in the day-care cases often did not believe the children. When children denied that they had been abused, they were not believed. It was only when, often under aggressive questioning, they began alleging abuse that they were believed. (This has been documented in many recent writings. See, for example, Dorothy Rabinowitz, "From the Mouths of Babes to a Jail Cell," and Philip Jenkins, *Moral Panic*.) The same principle operates in many quarters of the RM

movement. Only evidence supportive of the abuse claim is believed. There are many other resemblances between the day-care scandals and the RM movement: the "symptom" lists, the gullibility of early press reports. Such similarities are to be expected, since both movements are part of the same, exacerbated extension of the child-protection movement—a "national pathology," as Rabinowitz calls it (p. 63).

12. Fredrickson, *Repressed Memories*, p. 204.

13. "The group helps": Judith Lewis Herman, *Trauma and Recovery*, p. 221. "The stories got grosser": quoted in Bill Taylor, "Therapist Turned Patient's World Upside Down," p. C1.

14. Elvis Presley as abuse victim: The allegation is discussed in Julie Baumgold, "Midnight in the Garden of Good and Elvis," p. 66. Queen Elizabeth I: story by Jeremy Laurance, *Times* (London), 5 Feb. 1996, quoted in *False Memory Syndrome Foundation Newsletter*, March 1996, p. 5.

15. "Virtually every woman": Herman, *Trauma and Recovery*, p. 224. "So far, no one": Bass and Davis, *The Courage to Heal*, 1st ed., p. 22.

16. Quoted in the *False Memory Syndrome Foundation Newsletter*, Apr. 1994, p. 9.

17. Fifteen percent of male Vietnam veterans: according to the National Vietnam Veterans Adjustment Study, cited in Showalter, *Hystories*, p. 75. Tax-free income: Allan Young, *The Harmony of Illusions*, p. 213. "Veterans in emotional distress": Fred H. Frankel, "Discovering New Memories in Psychotherapy," p. 591. "Faced with any woman": Bonnie Burstow, *Radical Feminist Therapy*, quoted in Pendergrast, *Victims of Memory*, p. 452.

18. North and others, *Multiple Personalities, Multiple Disorders*, p. 20.

19. Ross, *The Osiris Complex*, pp. 68 ("suppressed"), 125 ("Why, scientifically"), 148–149 ("before I had heard," "taught me").

20. MPD and remote control: Hacking, *Rewriting the Soul*, p. 32. "The therapist finally tires of the game": Ganaway, "Historical Versus Narrative Truth," p. 214.

21. Both quotations: Sherry Turkle, "Laying Out the Moods," p. 6.

22. Lawrence Wright, *Remembering Satan*, pp. 42–43 ("I don't think so"), 57 ("Give me the responsibility").

23. Michael Jackson: These events are described in the *New York Times* review of Jackson's 1997 Honolulu concert: Jon Pareles, "Pop's Exiled King Pays State Visits with Pomp and Poses," p. C15.

24. Gloria Steinem, *Revolution from Within*, p. 318.

25. Margo Rivera, *Multiple Personality: A Training Model*, p. 6.

26. The case is described in Debbie Nathan, "Dividing to Conquer?" pp. 77–78.

27. Colin Ross quotations: *The Osiris Complex*, pp. xii–xiii. "The centerpiece for models": Putnam, *Diagnosis and Treatment of Multiple Personality Disorder*, p. viii.

28. "Why, in peaceful Winnipeg": Michael A. Simpson, "Gullible's Travels, or The Importance of Being Multiple," p. 92. MPD diagnoses at Sheppard Pratt: Donald R. Ross, "Discussion: An Agnostic Viewpoint on Multiple Personality Disorder," p. 134.

29. John Hochman, "M.P.D./D.I.D.: Time to Pull the P.L.U.G.," p. 10.

30. Corbett H. Thigpen and Hervey M. Cleckley, "On the Incidence of Multiple Personality Disorder," p. 63.

31. Putnam, *Diagnosis and Treatment of Multiple Personality Disorder*, p. 35.

32. Except where indicated, all quotations from Herbert Spiegel in this and the following three paragraphs are from an interview with the author. Spiegel has stated his views on Sybil and on MPD in general in a number of interviews, notably Mikkel Borch-Jacobsen's "Sybil—The Making of a Disease: An Interview with Dr. Herbert Spiegel."

33. Schreiber, *Sybil*, p. 130.

34. Schreiber, *Sybil*, p. 259.

35. A large number of RM patients resemble Sybil in this respect. In a survey of families who had contacted the False Memory Syndrome

Foundation, it was found that more than two-thirds of accusers believed they remembered abuse suffered before age four. Indeed, one-third claimed that they remembered being abused before age two (*False Memory Syndrome Foundation Newsletter*, Oct. 1997, p. 5). According to plentiful research, very few adults can remember much of anything that happened to them before age four.

36. Putnam, *Diagnosis and Treatment*, p. 35.

37. All quotations and information in this paragraph are from the unsigned *New York Times* article "Tapes Raise New Doubts About 'Sybil' Personalities," p. A1.

38. "When Dr. Wilbur wasn't there": quoted in the *False Memory Syndrome Foundation Newsletter*, Jan./Feb. 1999, p. 3. Sybil vacillated: "Tapes Raise New Doubts," p. A21. Royalty division: Robert S. Boynton, "Hidden Talents Dept.," p. 39.

Chapter 4: The Therapy

1. Richard P. Kluft, "Clinical Presentations of Multiple Personality Disorder," p. 607.

2. Putnam's lack of faith in reports of satanic ritual abuse: interview with author.

3. Putnam, *Diagnosis and Treatment of Multiple Personality Disorder*, p. 141.

4. "Their lifelong experience": Putnam, *Diagnosis and Treatment*, p. 136. "The most powerful": Richard P. Kluft, "Iatrogenic Creation of New Alter Personalities," p. 87.

5. Putnam, *Diagnosis and Treatment*, pp. 158 ("smoke out"), 90 ("Do you ever feel," "Can this other part").

6. Putnam, *Diagnosis and Treatment*, pp. 92 ("I would urge"), 86 ("though it may be").

7. Putnam, *Diagnosis and Treatment*, pp. 295 ("expect that new alters"), 121 ("Does this feeling").

8. Putnam, *Diagnosis and Treatment*, pp. 117 ("no one"), 211 ("I have received").

9. Putnam, *Diagnosis and Treatment*, p. 231.

10. This is the "sociocognitive" theory of MPD put forth by Nicholas P. Spanos in his 1994 essay "Multiple Personality Enactments and Multiple Personality Disorder." Spanos claims that the standard diagnostic interviews for MPD supply all the information a person would need in order to produce the basic signs of MPD.

11. "All of a sudden": Putnam, *Diagnosis and Treatment*, p. 131. The patient sometimes knows more: George Ganaway, interview with author. "Chameleon-like abilities": Putnam, *Diagnosis and Treatment*, p. 272.

12. Putnam, *Diagnosis and Treatment*, pp. 177 ("not uncommonly"), 214 ("flight into health"), 221 ("stonewalling," "poor prognostic sign").

13. Ross, *Multiple Personality Disorder*, p. 231.

14. Ralph Allison, with Ted Schwarz, *Minds in Many Pieces*, quoted in Pendergrast, *Victims of Memory*, p. 156.

15. Eighth hour of questioning; "interviewees must be prevented": Richard P. Kluft, "The Simulation and Dissimulation of Multiple Personality Disorder," p. 115. Examination methods like interrogation techniques: Simpson, "Gullible's Travels," p. 102. "I induced another personality": Eugene L. Bliss, "Multiple Personalities," p. 1392.

16. "The therapist may comment": Ross, *Multiple Personality Disorder*, p. 253. "Inner board meeting": Ross, *Multiple Personality Disorder*, p. 272. "Everybody listen": Kluft, "Varieties of Hypnotic Interventions in the Treatment of Multiple Personality," p. 236.

17. "Will whoever picked up the man": Bennett G. Braun, "The Uses of Hypnosis with Multiple Personality," p. 35. "I was able to access an alter": Richard P. Kluft, "Current Controversies Surrounding Dissociative Identity Disorder," p. 368.

18. Putnam, *Diagnosis and Treatment*, pp. 273–274.

19. Ross, *The Osiris Complex*, pp. 63–64.

20. Ross, *The Osiris Complex*, p. 64.

21. "Hard to describe": Ross, *The Osiris Complex*, p. 166. Quotations from Phillips: *The Magic Daughter*, pp. 135 ("That's cool"), 137 ("med'cine"). "Con artists": Ross, *Dissociative Identity Disorder*, p. 68.

Chapter 5: The Science

1. Frank W. Putnam and others, "The Clinical Phenomenology of Multiple Personality Disorder"; Colin A. Ross and others, "Multiple Personality Disorder: An Analysis of 236 Cases."

2. Data on duration of treatment with the reporting therapist were not given in the Ross study.

3. Hacking, *Rewriting the Soul*, p. 94.

4. Philip M. Coons and Victor Milstein, "Psychosexual Disturbances in Multiple Personality" (1986); Philip M. Coons, "Confirmation of Child Abuse in Child and Adolescent Cases of Multiple Personality Disorder and Dissociative Disorder Not Otherwise Specified" (1994).

5. Richard P. Kluft, "Multiple Personality Disorder, p. 162.

6. The Williams study is Linda Meyer Williams, "Recall of Childhood Trauma" (1994). Good critiques of it can be found in Ofshe and Watters, *Making Monsters*, pp. 305–309, and in Harrison G. Pope Jr., *Psychology Astray*, pp. 65–73. (As Pope notes, several studies have found that one-fourth to one-third of people, when asked, will fail to report *recent* experiences, and experiences that are not of an embarrassing nature—for example, a car accident.) "I didn't want to say it": Donna Della Femina and others, "Child Abuse: Adolescent Records vs. Adult Recall," p. 229. "A huge majority": Marlene Hunter, "President's Message," p. 1.

7. Ross, *Satanic Ritual Abuse*, p. 75. (He adds: "Often there will be a history of participation in child pornography, child prostitution, bestiality, and other highly deviant activities.") Likewise, Richard Kluft speculates that the average MP was abused twice a week, fifty weeks a year, for ten years ("The Treatment of Dissociative Disorder Patients," p. 98).

8. "The first generation": Ofshe and Watters, *Making Monsters*, p. 36. "That repetition of information": Daniel L. Schacter, *Searching for Memory*, p. 256.

9. Ulrich Neisser and N. Harsch, "Phantom Flashbulbs: False Recollections of Hearing the News about Challenger."

10. 1985 survey: G. E. Wyatt, "The Sexual Abuse of Afro-American and White American Women in Childhood." Citation of second Los Angeles study: S. D. Peters and others, "Prevalence." The prevalence studies are summarized by Spanos, *Multiple Identities and False Memories*, pp. 77–78.

11. "Amounts to negligence": Judith Lewis Herman, *Father-Daughter Incest*, p. 178.

12. "As yet, no psychiatric disorder": Putnam, *Dissociation in Children and Adolescents*, p. 45. Two groups' psychopathology rates approximately equal: M. R. Nash and others, "Long-Term Sequelae of Childhood Sexual Abuse." One 1994 study: P. G. Ney and others, "The Worst Combinations of Child Abuse and Neglect." "A substantial number": Eugene E. Levitt and Cornelia Maré Pinnell, "Some Additional Light on the Childhood Sexual Abuse–Pathology Axis." Likewise Joseph H. Beichtman and his colleagues, in a 1992 review of research on the long-term effects of childhood sexual abuse, conclude: "As yet there is insufficient evidence to confirm a relation between a history of childhood sexual abuse and a post-sexual abuse syndrome and multiple . . . personality disorder" (p. 101). As for the short-term effects of childhood sexual abuse, Kathleen A. Kendall-Tackett and her colleagues, in a 1993 review of the literature, report: "About two-thirds of the victimized children showed recovery within the first 12–18 months. The findings suggest the absence of any specific syndrome in children who have been sexually abused and no single traumatizing process" (p. 164).

13. Hacking, *Rewriting the Soul*, p. 65.

14. Ross, *Multiple Personality Disorder*, pp. 193 ("Strictly speaking"), 199 ("treated to integration"). In his 1997 revision of that book, Ross repeated that there were no outcome data (p. 247) but still asserted

that "all existing evidence indicates that the treatment of DID [MPD] is effective clinically" (p. 263). North and her colleagues, in their sober-minded *Multiple Personalities, Multiple Disorders,* summarize the situation: "No controlled studies investigating treatment effects have been done. This lack of systematic research permits development of unrealistic expectations . . . and of fantasies regarding outcome" (p. 180).

15. Cornelia B. Wilbur, "Multiple Personality and Child Abuse," p. 7. Rivera, *Multiple Personality: A Training Model,* p. 3. Bennett G. Braun, ed., *Treatment of Multiple Personality Disorder,* p. xvii.

16. Quoted in Penelope Mesic, "Presence of Minds," p. 126.

17. Interview with author. Kihlstrom reviews the research, and comments on the research that remains to be done, in his chapter "Dissociative Disorders" in the forthcoming third edition of the *Comprehensive Handbook of Psychopathology.*

18. "Over the next 10 years a substantial body": Ross, *Multiple Personality Disorder,* p. 311. "Over the next 10 years, the already substantial body": Ross, *Dissociative Identity Disorder,* p. 382. "The burden of proof": Ross, *Multiple Personality Disorder,* p. 62.

19. "Look, if we waited": quoted in Ofshe and Watters, *Making Monsters,* p. 30.

20. "No therapist": Putnam, *Diagnosis and Treatment of Multiple Personality Disorder,* p. 47. "I'm not a law-enforcement person": Dan Sexton, "Gaining Insights into the Complexity of Ritualistic Abuse," Eighth National Conference on Child Abuse and Neglect, quoted in Sherrill Mulhern, "Satanism and Psychotherapy," p. 146.

21. Kluft, "Clinical Presentations of Multiple Personality Disorder," pp. 609 ("intrapsychic structure"), 611 ("isomorphic" MPD), 621 ("latent MPD"), 623 ("private MPD," "secret MPD," "covert MPD"). Ross on MPD hiding beneath other diagnoses: *The Osiris Complex,* pp. 66–67, 121, 156, 158, 161, 232, 254, 294–295. Ross on AIDS–MPD connection: *Multiple Personality Disorder,* p. 94.

22. "If the 'entity'": Piper, *Hoax and Reality,* p. 7. "Sensitive alters": Richard P. Kluft, "Aspects of the Treatment of Multiple Personality

Disorder" (1984), quoted in Simpson, "Gullible's Travels," p. 108. Simpson quoting *Peter Pan:* "Gullible's Travels," p. 109.

23. "The charge of artifact": Ross, *Multiple Personality Disorder,* p. 61. "Violence against women": Judith L. Herman, "The Abuses of Memory," p. 4. "Overwhelming": Bass and Davis, *The Courage to Heal,* 3rd ed., p. 476.

24. "The gassing of the Kurds": Bass and Davis, *The Courage to Heal,* 3rd ed., p. 485. Blume comparing self to Tiananmen Square protestor: E. Sue Blume, "The Ownership of Truth" (1995), quoted in Pendergrast, *Victims of Memory,* p. 487. Letter to Loftus: Loftus and Ketcham, *The Myth of Repressed Memory,* p. 36. "To forget": Bass and Davis, *The Courage to Heal,* 3rd ed., p. 533.

25. "The scary miracle": Bass and Davis, *The Courage to Heal,* 3rd ed., p. 185. "Imagine all the women": Bass and Davis, *The Courage to Heal,* 3rd ed., p. 180. "How many pedophiles": Bass and Davis, *The Courage to Heal,* 1st ed., p. 169.

26. Herman, *Trauma and Recovery,* pp. 152 (go "underground," "We believe our patients"), 144–145 ("identification with the perpetrator"), 178 ("affirm a position").

Chapter 6: The Crisis

1. "An attempt to restore": Jeffrey S. Victor, "The Dynamics of Rumor—Panics about Satanic Cults," p. 232. "We are working with": Braun, presentation to Workshop on Identification and Treatment of Victims of Ritual Cult Abuse, Fifth International Conference on Multiple Personality/Dissociative States, Chicago, 1988, quoted in Mulhern, "Satanism and Psychotherapy," p. 166.

2. Five percent of clinicians reported 58 percent of SRA cases: Poole and others, "Psychotherapy and the Recovery of Memories of Childhood Sexual Abuse," p. 429. "Satanic cults": *Geraldo,* 19 Nov. 1987.

3. "People who believe": D. Corydon Hammond, quoted in Ofshe and Watters, *Making Monsters,* p. 193. A 1986 survey: cited by Nathan, "Dividing to Conquer?" p. 102.

4. "Legions of demons": Judith Spencer, *Suffer the Child,* quoted in North and others, *Multiple Personalities, Multiple Disorders,* p. 224. Harris's alters: Spencer, *Suffer the Child,* pp. xxiii–xxvii. Bromley estimate: David G. Bromley, "Satanism: The New Cult Scare," p. 62.

5. Kenneth Lanning speaking on the CBC *Fifth Estate* documentary "From the Mouths of Children," aired 12 Dec. 1995.

6. Ganaway, "Historical Versus Narrative Truth." Ganaway then expanded on this theory in his 1991 presentation to the American Psychological Association, "Alternative Hypotheses Regarding Satanic Ritual Abuse Memories." In his later writings "Transference and Countertransference Shaping Influences on Dissociative Syndromes and Hypnosis, Childhood Trauma, and Dissociative Identity Disorder," he continued to warn against solely trauma-dependent MPD theories, the use of hypnosis in recovered memory, and "alter"-focused treatment. The other information on Ganaway and Frank Putnam in this paragraph comes from interviews with the author.

7. Ganaway, personal communication.

8. "Pink flowers mean suicide": Braun, presentation to the Midwestern Conference on Child Sexual Abuse and Incest, University of Wisconsin, Madison, 12 Oct. 1992, quoted in Ofshe and Watters, *Making Monsters,* p. 248. Extended discussions of the cult theories of Braun, Ross, and Hammond can be found in this book and in Pendergrast's *Victims of Memory.*

9. "About twenty patients": Braun 1994 statement to Chicago *Tribune,* quoted in Matt Keenan, "The Devil and Dr. Braun," p. 10. Braun's precautions: Keenan, "The Devil and Dr. Braun," p. 10. The "rule of five": Keenan, "The Devil and Dr. Braun," p. 9. "Pimps, Pushers": Braun, presentation to Midwestern Conference on Child Sexual Abuse and Incest, University of Wisconsin, 12 Oct. 1992, quoted in Ofshe and Watters, *Making Monsters,* p. 247.

10. "Drugs including hallucinogens": Colin A. Ross, book proposal titled "CIA Mind Control," quoted in Pendergrast, *Victims of Memory,*

p. 194. Pendergrast on connection between Ross theory and John Marks book: *Victims of Memory*, p. 193. Ross speculation that MPD skepticism is part of CIA coverup: interview on CBC *Fifth Estate*, "Mistaken Identities."

11. The Hammond quotations in this paragraph are from Ofshe and Watters, *Making Monsters*, pp. 189 ("Alpha represents"), 195 ("Morticians are involved"), 187 ("I've finally decided").

12. Wright, *Remembering Satan*, p. 78.

13. Elizabeth S. Rose, "Surviving the Unbelievable."

Chapter 7: The Outcry

1. Spanos, *Multiple Identities and False Memories*, p. 296.

2. "A condition which": The definition, framed by memory researcher John Kihlstrom, appears in the FMS Foundation pamphlet "False Memory Syndrome: Frequently Asked Questions," p. 1. "We don't know the truth": interview with author.

3. "Close the dissociation services": Paul R. McHugh, "Multiple Personality Disorder," p. 6. "It is likely": Harold Merskey, "The Manufacture of Personalities," p. 26.

4. "In the UK": Ray Aldridge-Morris, *Multiple Personality*, p. 15. (The reply was from consulting psychiatrist Tony Armond.) "Some malignant being": August Piper Jr., "Multiple Personality Disorder and Criminal Responsibility," p. 36.

5. *Time* 1991 article: Christine Gorman, "Incest Comes Out of the Dark," 7 Oct. 1991. *Time* 1993 article: Leon Jaroff, "Lies of the Mind," 29 Nov. 1993. "Cathy said": Debbie Nathan, "Cry Incest," p. 162. Lawrence Wright article: "Remembering Satan," 17 and 24 May 1993. Frederick Crews article: "The Revenge of the Repressed," 17 Nov. and 1 Dec. 1994. Both Wright's and Crews's essays were later published in book form: Wright, *Remembering Satan*, 1994; Crews and others, *The Memory Wars*, 1995.

6. Cool case reported in New York: Helen Kennedy, "Devil Doc a Crock?" p. 8. "Sometimes Satan leaves rings of fire": Erickson, "Cool Recalls Ritual to Rid Her of Evil," A section, back page. Bur-

gus settlement reported in *New York Times:* Belluck, "'Memory' Therapy Leads to a Lawsuit," p. A1. "Kitsch": Wolcott on Harrison, "Dating Your Dad," pp. 32 ("trash"), 34 ("kitsch"). *New York Times* on Harrison: Christopher Lehmann-Haupt, "Life with Father," p. C18.

7. *Geraldo Live,* CNBC, 12 Dec. 1995.

8. As the present book is going to press, a new MPD memoir, *First Person Plural,* has been published, this one by a man, Cameron West. While MPD memoirs tend to be naive and lurid, West's book is a smooth, artful recitation, low on sex and high on liberal sentiments and brand-name consumer products. Chapter 1 opens: "I was lying on my back on our white Berber living room carpet, admiring the self-portraits in a luxuriously detailed book called *Rembrandt. The Human Form and Spirit.*" West's wife, Rikki, is in the kitchen, making dinner, "expertly slicing a Vidalia onion with an eight-inch Henckels knife." Soon West is cruising to his office in his Mercedes 450SLC. (Rikki only gets a Volvo.) Elsewhere West and Rikki sit on their deck, in their "forest-green Adirondack chairs," surveying their four-acre property. These comforts notwithstanding, West comes down with MPD. (As in the usual case, the first alter did not emerge until West went into psychotherapy.) But even then, things could be worse. He gets to do his journaling "on the redwood steps of our Jacuzzi," "in our glassed-in sunroom," while Rikki sits nearby, working her electric potter's wheel. Apart from its parading of the family's possessions, the book is notable for its sentimentality. At the opening, West lists his twenty-four alters—"my guys," as he tenderly calls them. Most of them are children. There's Davy, four years old ("He is sweet and sad"); Sharky ("he likes to share treats with the others"); Mozart, age six ("He is very quiet and fragile"); Switch, age eight ("Switch has his own sheriff's badge now, which he likes to wear around"); Anna, age four ("She loves a good cookie"); Dusty, age twelve (she "takes care of the little ones"); and Gail, another little girl, whom Dusty has taught to make bread, presumably in a name-brand oven. The older alters also tend toward the cuddly—Per, for example: "He is a poet, an artist. . . . He holds us tenderly in his arms and keeps us safe." Even Stroll, West's slut

alter—men apparently have them too—has joined the group hug.
Once a "sexual tool," now he has "changed his role to one of support for the younger alters." Despite repeated stays at the Ross Institute for Psychological Trauma at Charter Hospital, outside
Dallas—the institute is named for its founder–director, Colin Ross,
who supplies a blurb for the book ("*First Person Plural* is a great
achievement")—West still has not recovered by the time he writes
the final chapter. (Perhaps that is because he can still afford the
therapy.) As before, however, things aren't so bad: "Rikki quit her
job to stay home and watch out for us [him and his alters] and to
help me write this book. We take hikes and hold hands and talk
about Leonardo and Lautrec, Huck and Holmes, Beethoven and the
Beatles." The movie rights to *First Person Plural* have been sold, and
Robin Williams is to star in the film. The MPD movement is not
over yet.

Chapter 8: The Retrenchment

1. Bass and Davis, *The Courage to Heal*, 3rd ed., p. 527.

2. "One wonders what it is": Frank W. Putnam, *Dissociation in Children
   and Adolescents*, pp. 101–102. "The 'False Memory Syndrome'":
   Robert B. Rockwell, "One Psychiatrist's View of Satanic Ritual
   Abuse," p. 450. Pendergrast on Ross's fees: *Victims of Memory*, p.
   510. Ross quotations: Colin A. Ross, "President's Message," pp. 2
   ("has been identified"), 3 ("Some expert witnesses," "Therefore,
   therapists").

3. Nancy L. Hornstein, "President's Message," pp. 2 ("I refuse," "presupposing that clients' reports"), 7 ("First, do no harm").

4. Quotations from David Spiegel and Ganaway: interviews with
   author.

5. Ross, *Multiple Personality Disorder* (1989), pp. 3 ("is not an iatrogenic artifact"), 48 ("the world's leading Dissociative Disorders
   unit"), 199 ("three quarters of MPD patients"). Ross, *Dissociative
   Identity Disorder* (1997), pp. ix ("is not solely an iatrogenic artifact"), 48 ("the world's first Dissociative Disorders unit"), 56 ("the

great debt the field owes Dr. Braun"), 253 ("three quarters of Kluft's DID patients").

6. "The therapist must make explicit": Christine A. Curtois, *Healing the Incest Wound*, p. 141. "Never know": Christine A. Curtois, foreword to Judith L. Alpert, ed., *Sexual Abuse Recalled*, p. xiii. This is not all that Curtois has changed her mind about. In 1992, in her article "The Memory Retrieval Process in Incest Survivor Therapy," she recommended hypnosis, guided imagery, body work, and journaling as useful in recovering patients' forgotten abuse memories. In 1997, in a lecture to the NATO Advanced Study Institute called "Informed Clinical Practice and the Standard of Care: Guidelines for Treating Adults Who Report Delayed Memory for Past Trauma," she warned against these very procedures: "Hypnosis for memory retrieval, guided imagery, expressive therapies (art work, journaling, storytelling) . . . might lead to possible production of false memories" (quoted from conference proceedings in Felicity Goodyear-Smith, "Book Review: 'Recollections of Trauma: Scientific Research and Clinical Practice,'" *False Memory Syndrome Foundation Newsletter*, May 1988, pp. 12–13).

7. Bennett G. Braun, "Multiple Personality and Dissociative Disorders in Adult Survivors of Ritual Abuse," presentation to first annual conference of Believe the Children, 1993.

8. "The therapist should be uncomfortable": Ross, *Multiple Personality Disorder*, p. 251. "Acting out," "general adult unit": Ross, *Dissociative Identity Disorder*, p. 327.

9. "Painful or frightening experiences": Putnam, *Diagnosis and Treatment of Multiple Personality Disorder*, p. 227. "Blind probing": Frank W. Putnam, "Dr. Putnam's Response," in James A. Chu, "The Critical Issues Task Force Report: The Role of Hypnosis and Amytal Interviews in the Recovery of Traumatic Memories," p. 8. "Historical data": Richard P. Kluft, "Varieties of Hypnotic Interventions in the Treatment of Multiple Personality," p. 235. (In almost half those patients, hypnosis was also used in making the diagnosis of MPD.) "Fairly infrequent": Richard P. Kluft, "The Confirmation and

Disconfirmation of Memories of Abuse in DID Patients," p. 257. Hammond textbook quotations: D. Corydon Hammond, ed., *Handbook of Hypnotic Suggestions and Metaphors*, pp. 15–16 ("yes-set"), 17 ("foot-in-the-door technique"), 19 ("In hypnosis it is vitally important"). "It is vitally important for the therapist to seek to create neutral expectations": D. Corydon Hammond, "Hypnosis, False Memories, and Guidelines for Using Hypnosis with Potential Victims of Abuse," p. 117.

10. Seth R. Segall, "Misalliances and Misadventures in the Treatment of Dissociative Disorders," p. 385.

11. International Society for the Study of Dissociation, "Guidelines for Treating Dissociative Identity Disorder (Multiple Personality Disorder) in Adults," pp. 4 ("whole person," "single person," "not a collection"), 5 ("psychodynamically aware," "calming, soothing"), 6 ("Exclusive focus"), 8 ("help patients"), 9 ("a respectful neutral stance").

12. Kenneth S. Pope and Laura S. Brown, *Recovered Memories of Abuse*, pp. 208 ("burning questions"), 236 ("Any clinical case").

13. Nor, according to the ISSD guidelines, do they actually have to change their minds. As noted, the guidelines present current MPD therapy as a conservative, "ego-strengthening" enterprise. But the guidelines, for the most part, are descriptive, not prescriptive. They say what therapists do, not what they should do—an approach that yields a great deal of discussion on the order of "some believe . . . whereas others claim. . . ." In the process, many of the riskier methods of MPD therapy—the methods that produced the MPD epidemic, and that are the focus of the lawsuits—come into the discussion, and for the most part they are not disavowed. Though the patient is a whole person, a single person, still the therapist may address "the parts of the mind as if they were separate" (p. 4). Though marathon abreactions and extended hospitalization are warned against, still they may be used. Though the employment of hypnosis in diagnosing MPD is said to entail risks, it may nevertheless be helpful "when alternative diagnostic measures have failed to yield a definite conclusion" (p. 3). As for the place of hypnosis in

treatment, the guidelines list ego-strengthening functions—"calming, soothing, containment"—as its most common uses, but then they go on to list two further uses, the very two that have so discredited MPD therapy: the retrieval of memories and the calling up of alters. Even SRA claims, or what the guidelines blandly call "seemingly bizarre abuse experiences" (p. 9), get the on-the-one-hand-on-the-other-hand treatment: therapists are advised against taking "extreme positions on either side" (p. 9). Indeed, exorcism is not ruled out. At some point, the guidelines committee must have begun to worry that there was nothing they had excluded, for eventually they do definitively recommend against certain practices, for example, simulated breast-feeding (also bottle feeding) of the patient and inviting the patient into the therapist's home. Even here, though, there is a loophole, for the authors state at the outset that "these guidelines are not intended to replace the therapist's clinical judgment" (p. 1). In a letter printed in the *False Memory Syndrome Foundation Newsletter* in December 1998 (p. 3), Peter Barach, president of the ISSD, wrote that the guidelines "take strong positions against the excesses that some therapists committed" in treating MPD. One wonders what strong positions he is referring to.

14. Ross, *The Osiris Complex*, p. 50.

15. *False Memory Syndrome Foundation Newsletter*, Jan./Feb. 1999, p. 1.

16. "It's like they've taken us": unnamed psychiatrist quoted in Stephen Fried, "War of Remembrance," p. 69. "I will be implicated": Sue Grand, "Incest and the Intersubjective Politics of Knowing History," pp. 249–250.

17. All Barach statements: Peter M. Barach, "President's Message," p. 1. As the ISSD has shrunk in the last decade, the ISTSS has grown. Correspondingly, there are anecdotal reports that as the number of MPD diagnoses has fallen, the number of diagnoses of posttraumatic stress disorder has risen, and is rising still. Some observers are worried that the abuses—of patients, of science—involved in MPD therapy are not in fact dying out, but simply finding a new home under the heading of PTSD. Given the widespread closure of the

DD units and the withdrawal of financing for long-term therapy, it seems unlikely that PTSD therapy could flourish as MPD therapy did with those supports. But time will tell.

18. Allen Frances and Michael B. First, *Your Mental Health*, pp. 288 ("A good rule of thumb"), 289 ("If you are wondering," "may do more harm"), 290 ("We would recommend").

Chapter 9: The Effects

1. Simpson, "Gullible's Travels," p. 96.

2. The ISSD "Guidelines" modify this rule, but not by much. For the average patient, they recommend a *minimum* of two regular sessions per week, adding that "most therapists now see 3–5 years . . . as a minimum length of treatment, with many of the more complex patients requiring 6 or more years of outpatient psychotherapy" (p. 5). This is still a very costly project.

3. "Turn a $2000 eating disorder": quoted in Miriam Horn, "Memories Lost and Found," p. 55.

4. Interview with author.

5. Joe Sharkey, *Bedlam*, p. 11. Much of the information on the mental health hospitals in this and the following paragraphs comes from Sharkey's book.

6. *Houston Press* 1995 article: Bonnie Gangelhoff, "Devilish Diagnosis."

7. Pendergrast, *Victims of Memory*, pp. 176–177.

8. "I think organized crime"; mask hypothesis: quoted in Bonnie Gangelhoff, "Devilish Diagnosis," p. 16.

9. Quotations from Barden and Leggett: interviews with author.

10. G. A. Bonanno, "Remembering and Psychotherapy," p. 177.

11. One MPD-treater, David Calof, recommends that his patients "cut off" from their families but not confront them, not tell them why. The reason for this is that the family is likely to make the patient doubt her abuse memories. "You can't fight the family hypnosis," Calof says. He relates the cautionary tale of a patient who, having

been in therapy with him for five or six years, was "finally beginning to accept the reality of the horrendous, torturous child abuse she had endured" from her parents. She now told him that she wanted to confront her parents. He tried to dissuade her; she did it anyway, and came back to Calof protesting that the abuse memories were untrue: "She said, 'Why do you keep talking to me about stuff like that? My parents are wonderful, they could never have hurt me like that.'" Calof reports that it took him months to get her "back on track"—that is, back to believing that her parents had abused her. "Worse," he adds, "the alters who knew the truth were so enraged at her, they started cutting on her regularly for several weeks" (Calof, *Multiple Personality and Dissociation*, pp. 55–56).

12. "T........" ....'", D...........D......., *The C.......... ....* ed., p. 26. FMSF legal survey: summarized in Pamela Freyd, "Lessons from the False Memory Syndrome Foundation."

13. "I have worked": Ross, *Satanic Ritual Abuse*, p. 152. "Expressing doubt": Ross, *The Osiris Complex*, p. 149.

14. Quoted in Keenan, "The Devil and Dr. Braun," p. 10.

15. Crews, *The Memory Wars*, pp. 5 ("vulgar pseudoscience"), 114 ("we tell our patient"), 209 ("we must not believe what they say," "I remain unshakably firm").

16. Ganaway quotations: "Dissociative Disorders and Psychodynamic Theory." Haaken's views are presented in her "Sexual Abuse, Recovered Memory, and Therapeutic Practice" and "The Recovery of Memory, Fantasy, and Desire."

17. In 1997, in response to Barden's proposal and other initiatives, the Indiana state legislature passed a law requiring that mental health providers obtain informed consent from any prospective patient. (This includes informing the patient of the "risks and relative benefits of proposed treatments and alternative treatments.") Similar bills are being considered in a number of other state legislatures.

18. Interview with author.

19. "It's a know-nothing assault": interview with author. "A competent psychologist": American Psychological Association, "Questions and

Answers about Memories of Childhood Abuse," p. 3. The American
Psychological Association's wording should be compared with the
recent, unambiguous statement of the British Royal College of Psychiatrists: "Psychiatrists are advised to avoid engaging in any 'memory recovery techniques' which are based upon the expectation of
past sexual abuse of which the patient has no memory. Such 'memory recovery techniques' may include drug-mediated interviews,
hypnosis, regression therapies, guided imagery, 'body memories', literal dream interpretation and journaling. There is no evidence that
the use of consciousness-altering techniques, such as drug-mediated
interviews or hypnosis, can reveal . . . factual information about any
past experiences including childhood sexual abuse. . . . The psychiatrist should normally explore his or her doubts with the patient
about the accuracy of recovered memories of previously totally forgotten sexual abuse" (Royal College of Psychiatrists' Working
Group on Reported Recovered Memories of Child Sexual Abuse,
"Reported Recovered Memories of Child Sexual Abuse," pp.
663–664). Note that the Royal College does not support neutrality.
Instead, it urges the therapist to doubt the accuracy of recovered
memories and to discuss these doubts with the patient.

20. An interesting recent parallel has to do with the 1995 Holocaust
memoir *Fragments: Memories of a Wartime Childhood,* by the Swiss
writer Binjamin Wilkomirski. First published in Germany, the book
has since been translated into thirteen other languages. It has won a
number of literary prizes. Its American edition comes emblazoned,
on the cover, with the following endorsement from the *New York
Times Book Review:* "Extraordinary. He writes with a poet's vision, a
child's state of grace." Unfortunately, in 1998 legal records were produced to show that Wilkomirski—who claims that he was a Latvian
Jew and dates his memoir from 1939 to 1948, during which time he
says he survived detention in two Nazi prison camps—was born in
1941 to a Swiss Protestant mother and later adopted by a well-to-do
couple in Zurich. Wilkomirski has not yet responded to this con-
flicting information. According to the *New York Times* (Doreen
Caravajal, "A Holocaust Memoir in Doubt," p. E1), however, he has
said that his memories of the concentration camps were recon-

structed with the help of therapy. When asked by the *Times* about the veracity of the memoir, Wilkomirski's U.S. publisher, Arthur Samuelson, gave a statement that will sound familiar to students of the RM movement: "I believe he believes what's in the book, because it's largely based on recovered memory, and it's possible he's wrong" (quoted in Martin Arnold, "Making Books," p. E3). People concerned with the cause to which Wilkomirski has allied himself have responded less ambiguously. Konnilyn Feig, a Holocaust researcher, told the *Times*, "If it is not true, he has done a terrible thing to survivors" (quoted in Arnold, p. E3). That is, if the book is a fabrication, Wilkomirski will have given comfort—and ammunition—to Holocaust-deniers. In just the same way, false memories of abuse give comfort to those who would choose to ignore child abuse.

21. Wendy Kaminer, *I'm Dysfunctional, You're Dysfunctional*, p. 27.

22. "*You* didn't do anything": quoted in Pendergrast, *Victims of Memory*, p. 305. "Admit to the abuse": Yapko, *Suggestions of Abuse*, p. 184.

23. "We went every day": Roseanne Arnold, "A Star Cries Incest," p. 88. RM therapists becoming traumatized: see, for example, Karen W. Saakvitne, "Therapists' Responses to Dissociative Clients."

24. "When I was a little girl": Bass and Davis, *The Courage to Heal*, 3rd ed., p. 285. "I'll remember the good things": Gwendolyn Olinger Van Derbur, quoted in Marilyn Van Derbur Atler, "The Darkest Secret," p. 92. "I'd be lying on the altar": quoted in Pendergrast, *Victims of Memory*, p. 271.

25. Hacking's concern over effects of recovery literature: *Rewriting the Soul*, p. 238. "To make the word *incest*": Atler, "The Darkest Secret," p. 94.

Chapter 10: The Intellectuals

1. Bass and Davis, *The Courage to Heal*, 3rd ed., p. 138.

2. Helene Kafka, "Incestuous Sexual Abuse, Memory, and the Organization of the Self," p. 151.

3. Adrienne Harris, "False Memory? False Memory Syndrome? The So-Called False Memory Syndrome?," p. 178.

4. Joan Berzoff and Jaine Darwin, "Treatment of Character or Treatment of Trauma?," pp. 460 ("done by a 16-year-old alter"), 461 ("decline and further fragmentation"), 462 ("were able to co-construct," "were not able to move"), 463 ("aware that the diagnosis"—the quotation is from Kenneth Gergen).

Chapter 11: Women

1. Kaminer, *I'm Dysfunctional, You're Dysfunctional*, p. 89.

2. Schreiber, *Sybil*, p. 38.

3. Servant girls: Ellenberger, *The Discovery of the Unconscious*, p. 190. "Supreme monarchs of the royal blood": Burgus reports this on the *Frontline* documentary "The Search for Satan." Catherine the Great: Ofshe and Watters, *Making Monsters*, p. 240.

4. Ross, *The Osiris Complex*, p. 143.

5. "I went into the building": Ross, *Dissociative Identity Disorder*, p. 347. "The therapist will stay," "described in detail": Ross, *The Osiris Complex*, pp. 147–148.

6. "The Kids broke down": Jane Phillips, *The Magic Daughter*, p. 231. "Live theater," "like an ancient thaumaturge": quoted by North and others, *Multiple Personalities, Multiple Disorders*, p. 208.

7. Multiple Personality Consortium activities: Hacking, *Rewriting the Soul*, p. 37. Vynette Hamanne's Christmas presents: Monika Bauerlein, "The Mirror Cracked," p. 17.

8. Quoted in North and others, *Multiple Personalities, Multiple Disorders*, p. 187.

9. Adult experience of sexual assault in MPs: Putnam and others, "The Clinical Phenomenology of Multiple Personality Disorder," p. 289. "The sexual abuse explanation": Carol Tavris speaking on the *Frontline* documentary "Divided Memories."

10. Janice Haaken, "Sexual Abuse, Recovered Memory, and Therapeutic Practice," p. 122.

11. 1996 report: U.S. Department of Health and Human Services, *Executive Summary of the Third National Incidence Study of Child Abuse*

and Neglect (NIS–3), p. 10. Rivera report: Margo Rivera, *Multiple Personality: A Needs Assessment*, p. 4.

12. Quoted in Carol Tavris, *The Mismeasure of Woman*, pp. 320–321.

13. Nancy Scheper-Hughes and Howard F. Stein, "Child Abuse and the Unconscious in American Popular Culture," p. 342.

14. I. M. Lewis, *Ecstatic Religion*.

15. Ross, *The Osiris Complex*, p. 271.

16. "The word that strikes terror": Irvin D. Yalom, *Love's Executioner*, p. 213.

17. Quoted in Pendergrast, *Victims of Memory*, p. 90.

18. "To the extent": Seymour L. Halleck, "Dissociative Phenomena and the Question of Responsibility," p. 304. "It was Hyde": Robert Louis Stevenson, *The Strange Case of Dr. Jekyll and Mr. Hyde*, p. 46.

19. Yalom, *Love's Executioner*, pp. 213 ("everything else about her"), 221–222 ("In the middle of her dirge").

20. Yalom, *Love's Executioner*, pp. 225–226.

21. Yalom, *Love's Executioner*, p. 226.

22. Yalom, *Love's Executioner*, p. 228.

23. "Nous sommes toutes": Showalter, *Hystories*, p. 57. "A woman's language": Showalter, "Hysteria, Feminism, and Gender," p. 288.

Bibliography

Written Sources

Aldridge-Morris, Ray. *Multiple Personality: An Exercise in Deception.* Hillsdale, N.J.: Erlbaum, 1989.

Alpert, Judith L., ed. *Sexual Abuse Recalled: Treating Trauma in the Era of the Recovered Memory Debate.* Northvale, N.J.: Aronson, 1995.

American Medical Association, Council on Scientific Affairs. "Scientific Status of Refreshing Recollection by the Use of Hypnosis." *Journal of the American Medical Association,* 1985, *253*(13), 1918–1923.

American Psychiatric Association. *Diagnostic and Statistical Manual of Mental Disorders.* (4th ed., DSM-IV.) Washington, D.C.: American Psychiatric Association, 1994.

American Psychological Association. "Questions and Answers about Memories of Childhood Abuse." Washington, D.C.: American Psychological Association, 1995.

Angier, Natalie. "In the History of Gynecology, a Surprising Chapter." *New York Times,* 23 Feb. 1999, p. F5.

Armstrong, Louise. *Kiss Daddy Goodnight: Ten Years Later.* New York: Pocket Books, 1987.

Arnold, Martin. "Making Books." *New York Times,* 12 Nov. 1998, p. E3.

Arnold, Roseanne. "A Star Cries Incest." *People*, 7 Nov. 1991, pp. 84–88.

Atler, Marilyn Van Derbur. "The Darkest Secret." *People*, 10 June 1991, pp. 88–94.

Barach, Peter M. "President's Message." *ISSD News*, Jan. 1999, pp. 1–2, 8.

Bass, Ellen, and Laura Davis. *The Courage to Heal: A Guide for Women Survivors of Child Sexual Abuse*. (1st ed.) New York: Perennial Library, 1988.

Bass, Ellen, and Laura Davis. *The Courage to Heal: A Guide for Women Survivors of Child Sexual Abuse*. (3rd ed.) New York: HarperPerennial, 1994.

Bauerlein, Monika. "The Mirror Cracked." *City Pages*, 23 Aug. 1995, pp. 10–22.

Baumgold, Julie. "Midnight in the Garden of Good and Elvis." In Geoffrey C. Ward (ed.), *The Best American Essays, 1996*. Boston: Houghton Mifflin, 1996.

Beichtman, Joseph H., Kenneth J. Zucker, Jane E. Hood, Granville A. da Costa, Donna Akman, and Erika Cassavia. "A Review of the Long-Term Effects of Child Sexual Abuse." *Child Abuse and Neglect*, 1992, *16*, 101–118.

Belluck, Pam. "'Memory' Therapy Leads to a Lawsuit and Big Settlement." *New York Times*, 6 Nov. 1997, pp. A1, A13.

Berzoff, Joan, and Jaine Darwin. "Treatment of Character or Treatment of Trauma?" In Lewis M. Cohen and others (eds.), *Dissociative Identity Disorder*. Northvale, N.J.: Aronson, 1995.

Bliss, Eugene. "Multiple Personalities: A Report on 14 Cases with Implications for Schizophrenia and Hysteria." *Archives of General Psychiatry*, 1980, *37*, 1388–1397.

Blume, E. Sue. *Secret Survivors: Uncovering Incest and Its Aftereffects in Women*. New York: Ballantine, 1990.

Bonanno, G. A. "Remembering and Psychotherapy." *Psychotherapy*, 1990, *27*, 175–186.

Borch-Jacobsen, Mikkel. "Neurotica: Freud and the Seduction Theory." *October,* 1996, *76,* 15–43.

Borch-Jacobsen, Mikkel. "Sybil—The Making of a Disease: An Interview with Dr. Herbert Spiegel." *New York Review of Books,* 24 April 1997, pp. 60–64.

Boynton, Robert S. "Hidden Talents Dept." *New Yorker,* 28 Dec. 1998/4 Jan. 1999 (double issue), pp. 39–40.

Braun, Bennett G. "The Uses of Hypnosis with Multiple Personality." *Psychiatric Annals,* 1984, *14*(1), 34–40.

Braun, Bennett G., ed. *Treatment of Multiple Personality Disorder.* Washington, D.C.: American Psychiatric Press, 1986.

Braun, Bennett G. "Multiple Personality and Dissociative Disorders in Adult Survivors of Ritual Abuse." Presentation to Believe the Children annual conference, 1993.

Bromley, David G, "Satanism: The New Cult Scare." In James T. Richardson and others (eds.), *The Satanism Scare.* Hawthorne, N.Y.: Aldine de Gruyter, 1991.

Calof, David L., with Mary LeLoo. *Multiple Personality and Dissociation: Understanding Abuse, Incest, and MPD.* Park Ridge, Ill.: Parkside, 1993.

"Carla." [letter.] *Cutting Edge,* 1996, *7*(4), 8.

Carvajal, Doreen. "A Holocaust Memoir in Doubt." *New York Times,* 3 Nov. 1998, pp. E1, E8.

Cohen, Lewis M., Joan N. Berzoff, and Mark Elin, eds. *Dissociative Identity Disorder: Theoretical and Treatment Controversies.* Northvale, N.J.: Aronson, 1995.

Coons, Philip M. "Confirmation of Childhood Abuse in Child and Adolescent Cases of Multiple Personality Disorder and Dissociative Disorder Not Otherwise Specified." *Journal of Nervous and Mental Disease,* 1994, *182*(8), 461–464.

Coons, Philip M., and Victor Milstein. "Psychosexual Disturbances in Multiple Personality: Characteristics, Etiology, and Treatment." *Journal of Clinical Psychiatry,* 1986, *47*(3), 106–110.

Crews, Frederick. "The Revenge of the Repressed." *New York Review of Books*. Part 1: 17 Nov. 1994, pp. 54–60. Part 2: 1 Dec. 1994, pp. 49–58.

Crews, Frederick, and others. *The Memory Wars: Freud's Legacy in Dispute*. New York: New York Review of Books, 1995.

Curtois, Christine A. *Healing the Incest Wound: Adult Survivors in Therapy*. New York: Norton, 1988.

Curtois, Christine A. "The Memory Retrieval Process in Incest Survivor Therapy." *Journal of Child Sexual Abuse*, 1992, *1*(10), 15–29.

Curtois, Christine A. "Foreword." In Judith L. Alpert (ed.), *Sexual Abuse Recalled*. Northvale, N.J.: Aronson, 1995.

Davis, Laura. *The Courage to Heal Workbook: For Women and Men Survivors of Child Sexual Abuse*. New York: HarperCollins, 1990.

Della Femina, Donna, Catherine A. Yeager, and Dorothy Otnow Lewis. "Child Abuse: Adolescent Records vs. Adult Recall." *Child Abuse and Neglect*, 1990, *14*, 227–231.

Ellenberger, Henri F. *The Discovery of the Unconscious: The History and Evolution of Dynamic Psychiatry*. New York: Basic Books, 1970.

Erickson, Doug. "Cool Recalls Ritual to Rid Her of Evil." [Appleton-Neenah-Menasha, Wisconsin] *Post-Crescent*, 12 Feb. 1997, pp. A1–back page.

False Memory Syndrome Foundation. "Frequently Asked Questions." Philadelphia: False Memory Syndrome Foundation, 1995.

False Memory Syndrome Foundation Newsletter. Philadelphia: False Memory Syndrome Foundation, 1994–1999.

Forward, Susan, and C. Buck. *Betrayal of Innocence: Incest and Its Devastation*. New York: Penguin Books, 1988.

Frances, Allen, and Michael B. First. *Your Mental Health: A Layman's Guide to the Psychiatrist's Bible*. New York: Scribner, 1998.

Frankel, Fred H. "Discovering New Memories in Psychotherapy—Childhood Revisited, Fantasy, or Both?" *New England Journal of Medicine*, 1995, *333*(9), 591–594.

Fredrickson, Renee. *Repressed Memories: A Journey to Recovery from Sexual Abuse*. New York: Fireside/Parkside, 1992.

Freyd, Pamela. "Lessons from the False Memory Syndrome Foundation." Presentation to Massachusetts "Day of Contrition," Salem, 14 Jan. 1997.

Fried, Stephen. "War of Remembrance." *Philadelphia*, Jan. 1994, pp. 66–71, 149–157.

Ganaway, George K. "Historical Versus Narrative Truth: Clarifying the Role of Exogenous Trauma in the Etiology of MPD and Its Variants." *Dissociation*, 1989, *2*(4), 205–220.

Ganaway, George K. "Alternative Hypotheses Regarding Satanic Ritual Abuse Memories." Presentation to American Psychological Association, San Francisco, 19 Aug. 1991.

Ganaway, George K. "Dissociative Disorders and Psychodynamic Theory: Trauma Versus Conflict and Deficit." Presentation to conference "Memory and Reality: Emerging Crisis," Valley Forge, Pa., 17 Apr. 1993.

Ganaway, George K. "Transference and Countertransference Shaping Influences on Dissociative Syndromes." In Stephen Jay Lynn and Judith W. Rhue (eds.), *Dissociation: Clinical and Theoretical Perspectives*. New York: Guilford Press, 1994.

Ganaway, George K. "Hypnosis, Childhood Trauma, and Dissociative Identity Disorder: Toward an Integrative Theory." *International Journal of Clinical and Experimental Hypnosis*, 1995, *43*(2), 127–144.

Gangelhoff, Bonnie. "Devilish Diagnosis." *Houston Press*, 6–12 July 1995, pp. 8–16.

Gilman, Sander L., Helen King, Roy Porter, G. S. Rousseau, and Elaine Showalter. *Hysteria Beyond Freud*. Berkeley: University of California Press, 1993.

Goldstein, Eleanor, and Kevin Farmer. *True Stories of False Memories*. Boca Raton, Fla.: Upton, 1993.

Goodyear-Smith, Felicity. "Book Review: 'Recollections of Trauma: Scientific Research and Clinical Practice.'" *False Memory Syndrome Foundation Newsletter*, May 1998, pp. 11–13.

Gorman, Christine. "Incest Comes Out of the Dark." *Time*, 7 Oct. 1991, pp. 46–47.

Grand, Sue. "Incest and the Intersubjective Politics of Knowing History." In Judith L. Alpert (ed.), *Sexual Abuse Recalled*. Northvale, N.J.: Aronson, 1995.

Haaken, Janice. "Sexual Abuse, Recovered Memory, and Therapeutic Practice: A Feminist-Psychoanalytic Perspective." *Social Text*, 1994, *12*(3), 115–145.

Haaken, Janice. "The Recovery of Memory, Fantasy, and Desire: Feminist Approaches to Sexual Abuse and Psychic Trauma." *Signs*, 1996, *21*(4), 1069–1094.

Hacking, Ian. *Rewriting the Soul: Multiple Personality and the Sciences of Memory*. Princeton, N.J.: Princeton University Press, 1995.

Halleck, Seymour L. "Dissociative Phenomena and the Question of Responsibility." *International Journal of Clinical and Experimental Hypnosis*, 1990, *38*(4), 298–314.

Hammond, D. Corydon, ed. *Handbook of Hypnotic Suggestions and Metaphors*. New York: Norton, 1990.

Hammond, D. Corydon. "Hypnosis, False Memories, and Guidelines for Using Hypnosis with Potential Victims of Abuse." In Judith L. Alpert (ed.), *Sexual Abuse Recalled*. Northvale, N.J.: Aronson, 1995.

Harris, Adrienne. "False Memory? False Memory Syndrome? The So-Called False Memory Syndrome?" *Psychoanalytic Dialogues*, 1996, *6*(2), 155–187.

Harrison, Kathryn. *The Kiss*. New York: Random House, 1997.

Hart, B. "The Conception of Dissociation." *British Journal of Medical Psychology*, 1926, 6, 241–263.

Heaton, Jeanne Albronda, and Nona Leigh Wilson. *Tuning in Trouble: Talk TV's Destructive Impact on Mental Health*. San Francisco: Jossey-Bass, 1995.

Herman, Judith Lewis. *Father-Daughter Incest*. Cambridge, Mass.: Harvard University Press, 1981.

Herman, Judith Lewis. *Trauma and Recovery*. New York: Basic Books, 1992.

Herman, Judith Lewis. "The Abuses of Memory." *Mother Jones*, Mar./Apr. 1993, pp. 3–4.

Hochman, John. "M.P.D./D.I.D.: Time to Pull the P.L.U.G." *Southern California Psychiatrist*, Dec. 1996, p. 10.

Horn, Miriam. "Memories Lost and Found." *U.S. News and World Report*, 29 Nov. 1993, pp. 52–63.

Hornstein, Nancy L. "President's Message." *ISSD News*, Aug./Sept. 1995, pp. 2, 7.

Hunter, Marlene. "President's Message." *ISSD News*, June 1998, pp. 1, 5.

International Society for the Study of Dissociation, "Guidelines for Treating Dissociative Identity Disorder (Multiple Personality Disorder) in Adults." Northbrook, Ill.: International Society for the Study of Dissociation, 1997.

ISSMP&D News (from 1995, *ISSD News*). Skokie (later, Northbrook), Ill.: International Society for the Study of Multiple Personality and Dissociation (from 1995, International Society for the Study of Dissociation), 1994–1999.

Jaroff, Leon. "Lies of the Mind." *Time*, 29 Nov. 1993, pp. 52–59.

Jenkins, Philip. *Moral Panic: Changing Concepts of the Child Molester in Modern America*. New Haven, Conn.: Yale University Press, 1998.

Kafka, Helene. "Incestuous Sexual Abuse, Memory, and the Organization of the Self." In Judith L. Alpert (ed.), *Sexual Abuse Recalled*. Northvale, N.J.: Aronson, 1995.

Kaminer, Wendy. *I'm Dysfunctional, You're Dysfunctional: The*

Recovery Movement and Other Self-Help Fashions. Reading, Mass.: Addison-Wesley, 1992.

Keenan, Matt. "The Devil and Dr. Braun." *New City* (Chicago), 22 June 1995, pp. 9–11.

Kendall-Tackett, Kathleen, Linda Meyer Williams, and David Finkelhor. "Impact of Sexual Abuse on Children: A Review and Synthesis of Recent Empirical Studies." *Psychological Bulletin*, 1993, *113*, 164–180.

Kennedy, Helen. "Devil Doc a Crock?" *New York Daily News*, 13 Feb. 1997, p. 8.

Kenny, Michael G. *The Passion of Ansel Bourne: Multiple Personality in American Culture.* Washington, D.C.: Smithsonian Institution Press, 1986.

Kihlstrom, John F. "Dissociative Disorders." In Henry E. Adams and Patricia B. Sutker (eds.), *Comprehensive Handbook of Psychopathology.* (3rd ed.) New York: Plenum, forthcoming.

Kline, M. V. "A Note on 'Primate-Like' Behavior Induced Through Hypnosis: A Case Report." *Journal of General Psychology*, 1952, *81*, 125–131.

Kluft, Richard P. "Varieties of Hypnotic Interventions in the Treatment of Multiple Personality." *American Journal of Clinical Hypnosis*, 1982, *24*(4), 230–240.

Kluft, Richard P. "The Simulation and Dissimulation of Multiple Personality Disorder." *American Journal of Clinical Hypnosis*, 1987, *30*(2), 104–118.

Kluft, Richard P. "The Phenomenology and Treatment of Extremely Complex Multiple Personality Disorder." *Dissociation*, 1988, *1*, 47–58.

Kluft, Richard P. "Iatrogenic Creation of New Alter Personalities." *Dissociation*, 1989, *2*, 83–91.

Kluft, Richard P. "Multiple Personality Disorder." In A. Tasman and S. Goldfinger (eds.), *American Psychiatric Press Review of Psychiatry.* Vol. 10. Washington, D.C.: American Psychiatric Press, 1991.

Kluft, Richard P. "Clinical Presentations of Multiple Personality Disorder." *Psychiatric Clinics of North America,* 1991, *14*(3), 605–629.

Kluft, Richard P. "The Treatment of Dissociative Disorder Patients: An Overview of Discoveries, Successes, and Failures." *Dissociation,* 1993, 6, 87–101.

Kluft, Richard P. "The Confirmation or Disconfirmation of Memories of Abuse in DID Patients: A Naturalistic Clinical Study." *Dissociation,* 1995, 8(4), 253–258.

Kluft, Richard P. "Current Controversies Surrounding Dissociative Identity Disorder." In Lewis M. Cohen and others (eds.), *Dissociative Identity Disorder.* Northvale, N.J.: Aronson, 1995.

Laurence, Jean-Roch, and Campbell Perry. "Hypnotically Created Memory Among Highly Hypnotizable Subjects." *Science,* 1983, 222, 523–524.

Lehmann-Haupt, Christopher. "Life with Father." *New York Times,* 27 Feb. 1997, p. C18.

Levitt, Eugene E., and Cornelia Maré Pinnell. "Some Additional Light on the Childhood Sexual Abuse–Pathology Axis." *International Journal of Clinical and Experimental Hypnosis,* 1995, 43(2), 145–162.

Lewis, I. M. *Ecstatic Religion.* New York: Routledge, 1987.

Loftus, Elizabeth, and Katherine Ketcham. *The Myth of Repressed Memory: False Memories and Allegations of Sexual Abuse.* New York: St. Martin's Press, 1994.

Marks, John. *The Search for the "Manchurian Candidate": The CIA and Mind Control.* New York: Times Books, 1979.

Masson, Jeffrey Moussaieff. *The Assault on Truth: Freud's Suppression of the Seduction Theory.* New York: Farrar, Straus & Giroux, 1984.

McHugh, Paul R. "Multiple Personality Disorder." *Harvard Mental Health Letter,* 1993, 10(3), 4–6.

McHugh, Paul R. "Foreword." In August Piper Jr., *Hoax and Reality.* Northvale, N.J.: Aronson, 1997.

Merskey, Harold. "The Manufacture of Personalities: The Production of Multiple Personality Disorder." In Lewis M. Cohen and others (eds.), *Dissociative Identity Disorder*. Northvale, N.J.: Aronson, 1995.

Mesic, Penelope. "Presence of Minds." *Chicago*, Sept. 1992, pp. 101–103, 122–128, 133.

Micale, Mark S. *Approaching Hysteria: Disease and Its Interpretations*. Princeton, N.J.: Princeton University Press, 1995.

Mulhern, Sherrill. "Satanism and Psychotherapy." In James T. Richardson and others (eds.), *The Satanism Scare*. Hawthorne, N.Y.: Aldine de Gruyter, 1991.

Nash, M. R., T. L. Hulsey, M. C. Sexton, T. L. Harralson, and W. Lambert. "Long-Term Sequelae of Childhood Sexual Abuse: Perceived Family Environment, Psychopathology, and Dissociation." *Journal of Consulting and Clinical Psychology*, 1993, *61*, 276–283.

Nathan, Debbie. "Cry Incest." *Playboy*, Oct. 1992, pp. 84, 86, 88, 162, 164.

Nathan, Debbie. "Dividing to Conquer? Women, Men, and the Making of Multiple Personality Disorder." *Social Text*, 1994, *12*(3), 77–114.

Neisser, Ulrich, and N. Harsch. "Phantom Flashbulbs: False Recollections of Hearing the News About Challenger." In E. Winograd and Ulrich Neisser (eds.), *Affect and Accuracy in Recall: Studies of "Flashbulb" Memories*. New York: Cambridge University Press, 1992.

Nelson, Eric L., and Paul Simpson. "First Glimpse: An Initial Examination of Subjects Who Have Rejected Their Recovered Visualizations as False Memories." *Issues in Child Abuse Accusations*, 1994, 6(3), 123–133.

Ney, P. G., T. Fung, and A. R. Wickett. "The Worst Combinations of Child Abuse and Neglect." *Child Abuse and Neglect*, 1994, *18*, 705–714.

North, Carol S., JoEllyn M. Ryall, Daniel A. Ricci, and Richard D. Wetzel. *Multiple Personalities, Multiple Disorders: Psychiatric Classification and Media Influence*. Oxford: Oxford University Press, 1993.

Ofshe, Richard, and Ethan Watters. *Making Monsters: False Memories, Psychotherapy, and Sexual Hysteria*. New York: Scribner, 1994.

Pareles, Jon. "Pop's Exiled King Pays State Visits with Pomp and Poses." *New York Times*, 6 Jan. 1997, pp. C11, C15.

Pendergrast, Mark. *Victims of Memory: Sex Abuse Accusations and Shattered Lives*. (2nd ed.) Hinesburg, Vt.: Upper Access, 1996.

Peters, S. D., G. E. Wyatt, and D. Finkelhor. "Prevalence." In D. Finkelhor, S. Araji, L. Baron, A. Browne, S. D. Peters, and G. E. Wyatt (eds.), *A Sourcebook on Child Sexual Abuse*. Thousand Oaks, Calif.: Sage, 1986.

Petersen, Betsy. *Dancing with Daddy: A Childhood Lost and a Life Regained*. New York: Bantam Books, 1992.

Phillips, Jane. *The Magic Daughter: A Memoir of Living with Multiple Personality Disorder*. New York: Viking, 1995.

Piper, August, Jr. "Multiple Personality Disorder and Criminal Responsibility: Critique of a Paper by Elyn Saks." *Journal of Psychiatry and Law*, 1994, 22, 7–49.

Piper, August, Jr. *Hoax and Reality: The Bizarre World of Multiple Personality Disorder*. Northvale, N.J.: Aronson, 1997.

Poole, Debra A., D. Stephen Lindsay, Amina Memon, and Ray Bull. "Psychotherapy and the Recovery of Memories of Childhood Sexual Abuse: U.S. and British Practitioners' Opinions, Practices, and Experiences." *Journal of Consulting and Clinical Psychology*, 1995, 63(3), 426–437.

Pope, Harrison G., Jr. *Psychology Astray: Fallacies in Studies of "Repressed Memory" and Childhood Trauma*. Boca Raton, Fla.: Upton, 1997.

Pope, Harrison G., Jr., Paul S. Oliva, James I. Hudson, J. Alexander Bodkin, and Amanda J. Gruber. "Attitudes Toward DSM-IV Dissociative Disorder Diagnoses Among Board-Certified American Psychiatrists." *American Journal of Psychiatry*, 1999, *156*(2), 321–323.

Pope, Kenneth S., and Laura S. Brown. *Recovered Memories of Abuse: Assessment, Therapy, Forensics*. Washington, D.C.: American Psychological Association, 1996.

Porter, Roy. "The Body and the Mind, the Doctor and the Patient." In Sander L. Gilman and others, *Hysteria Beyond Freud*. Berkeley: University of California Press.

Putnam, Frank W. *Diagnosis and Treatment of Multiple Personality Disorder*. New York: Guilford Press, 1989.

Putnam, Frank W. "Dr. Putnam's Response." In James A. Chu, "The Critical Issues Task Force Report: The Role of Hypnosis and Amytal Interviews in the Recovery of Traumatic Memories." *ISSMP&D News*, June 1992, pp. 7–8.

Putnam, Frank W. *Dissociation in Children and Adolescents: A Developmental Perspective*. New York: Guilford Press, 1997.

Putnam, Frank W., Juliet J. Guroff, Edward K. Silberman, Lisa Barban, and Robert Post. "The Clinical Phenomenology of Multiple Personality Disorder: Review of 100 Recent Cases." *Journal of Clinical Psychiatry*, 1986, *47*(6), 285–293.

Rabinowitz, Dorothy. "From the Mouths of Babes to a Jail Cell." *Harper's Magazine*, May 1990, pp. 52–63.

Richardson, James T., Joel Best, and David G. Bromley, eds. *The Satanism Scare*. Hawthorne, N.Y.: Aldine de Gruyter, 1991.

Rivera, Margo. *Multiple Personality: A Needs Assessment*. Toronto: Education/Dissociation, 1992.

Rivera, Margo. *Multiple Personality: A Training Model*. Toronto: Education/Dissociation, 1992.

Rockwell, Robert B. "One Psychiatrist's View of Satanic Ritual Abuse." *Journal of Psychohistory*, 1994, *21*(4), 443–460.

Rose, Elizabeth S. "Surviving the Unbelievable." *Ms.*, Jan./Feb. 1993, pp. 40–45.

Ross, Colin A. *Multiple Personality Disorder: Diagnosis, Clinical Features, and Treatment.* New York: Wiley, 1989.

Ross, Colin A. *The Osiris Complex: Case-Studies in Multiple Personality Disorder.* Toronto: University of Toronto Press, 1994.

Ross, Colin A. "President's Message." *ISSMP&D News*, Apr. 1994, pp. 1–3.

Ross, Colin A. *Satanic Ritual Abuse: Principles of Treatment.* Toronto: University of Toronto Press, 1995.

Ross, Colin A. *Dissociative Identity Disorder: Diagnosis, Clinical Features, and Treatment of Multiple Personality.* (2nd rev ed of *Multiple Personality Disorder.*) New York: Wiley, 1997.

Ross, Colin A., G. Ron Norton, and Kay Wozney. "Multiple Personality Disorder: An Analysis of 236 Cases." *Canadian Journal of Psychiatry*, 1989, *34*, 413–418.

Ross, Donald R. "Discussion: An Agnostic Viewpoint on Multiple Personality Disorder." *Psychoanalytic Inquiry*, 1992, *12*(1), 124–138.

Rousseau, G. S. "'A Strange Pathology': Hysteria in the Early Modern World, 1500–1800." In Sander L. Gilman and others (eds.), *Hysteria Beyond Freud.* Berkeley: University of California Press.

Royal College of Psychiatrists' Working Group on Reported Recovered Memories of Child Sexual Abuse. "Reported Recovered Memories of Child Sexual Abuse: Recommendations for Good Practice and Implications for Training, Continuing Professional Development and Research." *College Psychiatric Bulletin*, 1997, *21*, 663–665.

Saakvitne, Karen W. "Therapists' Responses to Dissociative Clients: Countertransference and Vicarious Traumatization." In Lewis M. Cohen and others, *Dissociative Identity Disorder.* Northvale, N.J.: Aronson, 1995.

Schacter, Daniel L. *Searching for Memory: The Brain, the Mind, and the Past*. New York: Basic Books, 1996.

Scheper-Hughes, Nancy, and Howard Stein. "Child Abuse and the Unconscious in American Popular Culture." In Nancy Scheper-Hughes (ed.), *Child Survival: Anthropological Perspectives on the Treatment and Maltreatment of Children*. Dordrecht, Netherlands: Reidel, 1987.

Schreiber, Flora Rheta. *Sybil*. New York: Warner Books, 1974.

Segall, Seth Robert. "Misalliances and Misadventures in the Treatment of Dissociative Disorders." In Lewis M. Cohen and others (eds.), *Dissociative Identity Disorder*. Northvale, N.J.: Aronson, 1995.

Sharkey, Joe. *Bedlam: Greed, Profiteering, and Fraud in a Mental Health System Gone Crazy*. New York: St. Martin's Press, 1994.

Shorter, Edward. *From Paralysis to Fatigue: A History of Psychosomatic Illness in the Modern Era*. New York: Free Press, 1992.

Showalter, Elaine. "Hysteria, Feminism, and Gender." In Sander L. Gilman and others, *Hysteria Beyond Freud*. Berkeley: University of California Press, 1993.

Showalter, Elaine. *Hystories: Hysterical Epidemics and Modern Culture*. New York: Columbia University Press, 1997.

Simpson, Michael A. "Gullible's Travels, or The Importance of Being Multiple." In Lewis M. Cohen and others (eds.), *Dissociative Identity Disorder*. Northvale, N.J.: Aronson, 1995.

Smith, Michelle, and Lawrence Pazder. *Michelle Remembers*. New York: Pocket Books, 1980.

Spanos, Nicholas P. "Multiple Identity Enactments and Multiple Personality Disorder: A Sociocognitive Perspective." *Psychological Bulletin*, 1994, *116*, 143–165.

Spanos, Nicholas P. *Multiple Identities and False Memories: A Sociocognitive Perspective*. Washington, D.C.: American Psychological Association, 1996.

Spencer, Judith. *Suffer the Child*. New York: Pocket Books, 1989.

Steinem, Gloria. *Revolution from Within: A Book of Self-Esteem*. New York: Little, Brown, 1993.

Stevenson, Robert Louis. *The Strange Case of Dr. Jekyll and Mr. Hyde*. New York: Dover, 1991. (Originally published 1886.)

"Tapes Raise New Doubts about 'Sybil' Personalities." *New York Times*, 19 Aug. 1998, p A21.

Tavris, Carol. *The Mismeasure of Woman*. New York: Simon & Schuster, 1992.

Taylor, Bill. "Therapist Turned Patient's World Upside Down." *Toronto Star*, 19 May 1992, p. C1.

Taylor, W. S., and Mabel F. Martin. "Multiple Personality." *Journal of Abnormal and Social Psychology*, 1944, 39(3), 281–300.

Thigpen, Corbett H., and Hervey M. Cleckley. "A Case of Multiple Personality." *Journal of Abnormal and Social Psychology*, 1954, 49, 135–151.

Thigpen, Corbett H., and Hervey M. Cleckley. *The Three Faces of Eve*. New York: McGraw-Hill, 1957.

Thigpen, Corbett H., and Hervey M. Cleckley. "On the Incidence of Multiple Personality Disorder: A Brief Communication." *International Journal of Clinical and Experimental Hypnosis*, 1984, 32(2), 63–66.

Thigpen, Corbett H., and Hervey M. Cleckley. *The Three Faces of Eve*. (rev ed.) Privately published, 1992. Available from The Three Faces of Eve, P.O. Box 2619, Augusta, GA 30904.

Tickner, Lisa. *The Spectacle of Women*. Chicago: University of Chicago Press, 1988.

The Troops, for Truddi Chase. *When Rabbit Howls*. New York: Jove, 1990.

Turkle, Sherry. "Laying Out the Moods." *London Review of Books*, 19 Mar. 1998, pp. 3–6.

U.S. Department of Health and Human Services. *Executive Summary of the Third National Incidence Study of Child Abuse and Neglect* (NIS-3). Washington, D.C.: U.S. Department of Health and Human Services, 1996.

Victor, Jeffrey S. "The Dynamics of Rumor—Panics About Satanic Cults." In James T. Richardson and others (eds.), *The Satanism Scare*. Hawthorne, N.Y.: Aldine de Gruyter, 1991.

Victor, Jeffrey S. *Satanic Panic: The Creation of a Contemporary Legend*. Chicago: Open Court, 1993.

West, Cameron. *First Person Plural: My Life as a Multiple*. New York: Hyperion, 1999.

Wilbur, Cornelia B. "Multiple Personality and Child Abuse: An Overview." *Psychiatric Clinics of North America*, 1984, 7(1), 3–7.

Wilkomirski, Binjamin. *Fragments: Memories of a Wartime Childhood*. Trans. Carol Brown Janeway. New York: Schocken Books, 1995.

Williams, Linda Meyer. "Recall of Childhood Trauma: A Prospective Study of Women's Memories of Child Sexual Abuse." *Journal of Consulting and Clinical Psychology*, 1994, 62(6), 1167–1176.

Wolcott, James. "Dating Your Dad." *New Republic*, 31 Mar. 1997, pp. 32–36.

Wright, Lawrence. "Remembering Satan." *New Yorker*, Part 1: 17 May 1993, pp. 60–81; Part 2: 24 May 1993, pp. 54–76.

Wright, Lawrence. *Remembering Satan*. New York: Knopf, 1994.

Wyatt, G. E. "The Sexual Abuse of Afro-American and White American Women in Childhood." *Child Abuse and Neglect*, 1985, 9, 507–519.

Yalom, Irvin D. *Love's Executioner, and Other Tales of Psychotherapy*. New York: Basic Books, 1989.

Yapko, Michael D. *Suggestions of Abuse: True and False Memories of Childhood Sexual Trauma*. New York: Simon & Schuster, 1994.

Young, Allan. *The Harmony of Illusions: Inventing Post-Traumatic Stress Disorder*. Princeton, N.J.: Princeton University Press, 1995.

Television Documentaries

"Devil's Advocate." Prod. Katy Smyser. Correspondent Victoria
    Corderi. NBC, *Dateline*, 27 Oct. 1998.

"Divided Memories." Prod. and dir. Ofra Bikel. WGBH, *Frontline*,
    4 and 11 Apr. 1995.

"From the Mouths of Children." Prod. and dir. Michelle Métivier.
    CBC, *The Fifth Estate*, 12 Dec. 1995.

"Mistaken Identities." Prod. and dir. Michelle Métivier. CBC, *The
    Fifth Estate*, 9 Nov. 1993.

"The Search for Satan." Prod. and dir. Ofra Bikel and Rachel
    Dretzin. WGBH, *Frontline*, 24 Oct. 1995.

Acknowledgments

This book is a greatly expanded version of an essay, "The Politics of Hysteria," that was published in the *New Yorker* in 1998. My first thanks are to Elizabeth Carlson, who spent many hours going over with me a story that she would surely have preferred to forget. I am also grateful to Lisha Carlson, Elizabeth's daughter, who participated in these conversations.

The following people gave me interviews: Christopher Barden, Elizabeth Bowman, George Ganaway, Marche Isabella, John Kihlstrom, Richard Kluft, Jack Leggett, Frank Putnam, David Spiegel, and Herbert Spiegel. The following answered questions, supplied materials, and/or checked the manuscript: Ofra Bikel, Mikkel Borch-Jacobsen, Zachary Bravos, Patricia Burgus, Frederick Crews, Rachel Dretzin, Pamela Freyd, George Ganaway, Michelle Galindo, Eleanor Goldstein, Janice Haaken, Stephen Kirschner, Anita Lipton, Lloyd de Mause, Michelle Métivier, David Patton, Mark Pendergrast, Harrison Pope Jr., August Piper Jr., Nancy Scheper-Hughes, Mary Shanley, Skip Simpson, Mark Smith, Katie Spanuello, and Lawrence Wright. Pamela Freyd of the False Memory Syndrome Foundation repeatedly sent me materials that I needed. The officers and staff of the International Society for the Study of Dissociation also responded to my requests for documents and information, even after it was clear, from the *New Yorker* essay, that I did not share their view of multiple personality disorder. The same is true for others named above. Some of the people who helped me support my conclusions about MPD; others strongly disagree with me. I thank all of them for their time and trouble.

I thank the staff of the *New Yorker*: Tina Brown, who assigned the article, Dorothy Wickenden, who advised on it; Ted Katauskas, Greg Villepique, and Anne Mortimer-Maddox, who fact-checked it; and above all, Deborah Garrison, who edited it. For assistance with the book version I am grateful to Alan Rinzler, executive editor, and Katie Crouch, editorial assistant, of Jossey-Bass, and to my friend and agent Robert Cornfield.

The Author

Joan Acocella is a staff writer for the *New Yorker*. She is the author of *Mark Morris* (1993) and the editor of *The Diary of Vaslav Nijinsky* (1999). She coauthored the textbook *Abnormal Psychology: Current Perspectives*, now in its eighth edition (1999). She has been a Guggenheim fellow and is currently a fellow of the New York Institute for the Humanities.

Index